Wholly Connected
Five Pathways for the Return to True Community

EVE CALLAWAY WILLSON

WHOLLY CONNECTED: *Five Pathways for the Return to True Community*
Copyright © 2019 Eve Callaway Willson

All rights reserved. This book may not be reproduced in whole or in part, without written permission from the author, except by a reviewer who may quote brief passages. Nor may any part of this book be stored in a retrieval system, or transmitted in any form or by any means electronic, mechanical, photocopying, recording, scanning, etc.

For permissions and other inquiries, contact True Center Publishing at P.O. Box 1241, Woodstock, GA 30188. To learn more about True Center, visit our website: http://truecenterwoodstock.org.

Mandala designs on cover and interior © Ken Callaway
The Spiral Path of Connection graphic © Dawn Richerson

ISBN 978-1-7332900-0-5 Paperback
ISBN 978-1-7332900-1-2 E-Book

LCCN 2019913466

Printed in the United States of America

Dedicated to my beloved grandson, Barrett.
May you ever BE wholly connected.

As You Begin Your Journey

How to Use This Book

The book is organized into five sections. Each section corresponds to one of five unfolding pathways of connection along The Spiral Path of Connection. Each of these sections are further divided into three chapters each. These chapters provide an overview of the particular pathway followed by ways to experience greater connection along this pathway and practical steps for individuals and communities.

The five primary pathways to greater connection and community spiral out from the True Self at center. Making connections along these pathways leads us into a greater experience of community within and without. Each section concludes with a list of powerful questions for deeper connection. These questions are designed to facilitate inner reflection and elicit ideas for living a fuller, more connected life. The questions can also be used in group settings to spark conversations that nurture connections to a thriving community.

Where to Begin

Cultivating connection to community takes focused intent and effort, yet there are so many ways to begin. Begin by using this book as a guide to connection. The five pathways point the way to True Community with practical ideas for deepening connections to self, family and friends, the larger community, nature, and the global community.

The journey begins within. It is important that you begin at the center of the spiral with a strong connection to your True Self. From there, you may choose to focus on one or two connection pathways—or you may explore all five connection pathways. As you explore, remember your vital contribution to connected communities supports a more empowered, uplifting experience of life for yourself and others.

Contents

The Spiral Path of Connection...........................i
The Five Pathways ii
Characteristics of a Thriving Community.....................v
Introduction: Wholly Connected vii

1. The True Self
Remembering Who You Are 2
Going Deeper: Seeing with New Eyes..........................15
Practices for Connection: The True Self 25
21 Questions for Deeper Reflection 32

2. Family and Friends
Close Connections and Community 34
Going Deeper: Strengthening Bonds.............................45
Practices for Connection: Family & Friends.................62
21 Questions for Deeper Reflection 68

3. The Larger Community
Local Connections...72
Going Deeper: Intentional Connections........................88
Practices for Connection: The Larger Community 97
21 Questions for Deeper Reflection 100

4. Nature
Connecting with the Heart of Nature 104
Going Deeper: Nature and Community 112
Practices for Connection: Nature 120
21 Questions for Deeper Reflection 127

5. The Global Community
Global Awareness...130
Going Deeper: Connecting as a Global Citizen 146
Practices for Connection: The Global Community 153
21 Questions for Deeper Reflection 157

In Closing: An Invitation to Opening............................159
Acknowledgments...161
About True Center 162
About the Author 163

The Spiral Path of Connection

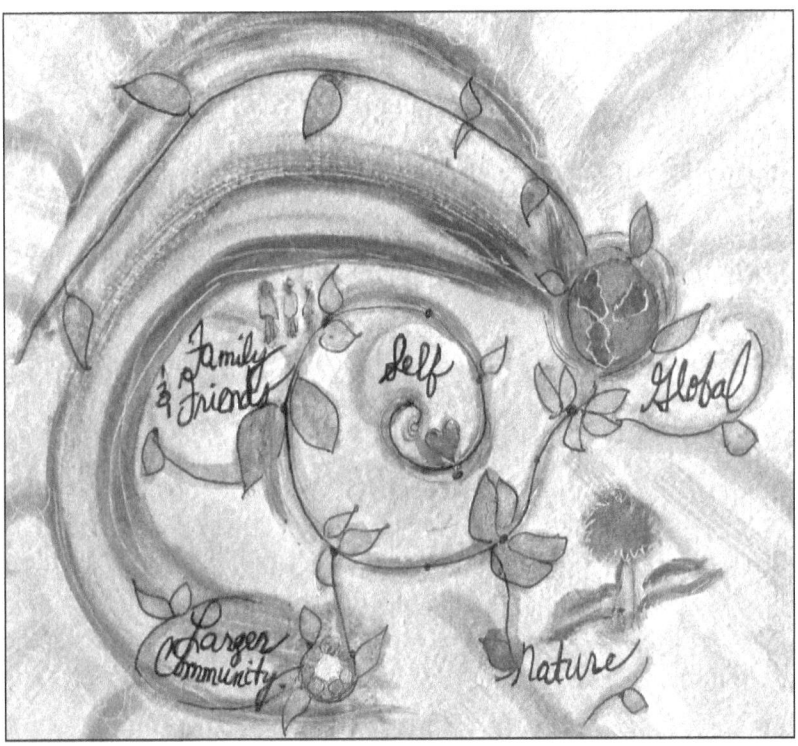

THE SPIRAL PATH OF CONNECTION includes five pathways for a return to True Community. These pathways of connection include:

- The True Self
- Family and Friends
- The Larger Community
- Nature
- The Global Community

The Five Pathways

As we travel The Spiral Path together, we will explore five pathways of connection. Each pathway supports deeper connection and a return to True Community. As you strengthen and expand along each pathway that unfurls from the center, you experience greater thriving and fulfillment in your everyday life.

The description of each pathway that follows will enhance your understanding of the concepts we will explore in this book. The five pathways along The Spiral Path of Connection include: the True Self, Family and Friends, the Larger Community, Nature, and the Global Community.

The True Self

Your connection to your True Self begins with greater self-awareness, self-acceptance, and self-love. Self-connection leads to compassion for others. If you do not love yourself, it is impossible to connect with others in ways that are meaningful and satisfying. You must reconnect with yourself in a conscious way to develop greater compassion and empathy, which then allows you to connect to True Community. There are many ways to connect with your True Self. Along this pathway, we will explore practical tips for deeper connection to the self and suggest simple practices and questions for reflection that will help you cultivate compassion and love for yourself.

Family and Friends

As you cultivate a deeper connection with yourself, that love naturally expands outward to include others with whom you are in close relationships. As your compassion for yourself grows, you will notice that you have a deeper understanding of your own needs and the needs of others. Communicating and interacting with others in more loving, compassionate, and peaceful ways then comes more naturally.

Exploring this pathway will help you identify specific ways to cultivate closer connections with your family member and friends.

The Larger Community

The larger community refers to the communities we live in and interact in on a day-to-day basis. The larger community might include your neighborhood or local town or community, churches or religious organizations, schools and educational institutions, and local government bodies. It can include places where you shop or come together with others as well as social interactions and social integration. Along this pathway, you'll discover practical tips and ideas for getting involved and creating a more meaningful life as you contribute to the greater good of your community, helping to make it more viable and resilient. We will consider how you can strengthen the bonds of connection that exist in your local environment and with the people and places you connect to in your daily life.

Nature

In our busy lives, it sometimes seems that we have forgotten that we live in the natural world and are an integral part of it. The consequences of seeing ourselves as separate from the natural world we live in include pollution and waste, the misuse or depletion of natural resources, disregard for the environment, and cruelty to animals. This pathway encourages you to connect with the natural world and to live *with* it rather than seeing it as separate or something to be dominated and controlled. Connecting with nature can be as simple as noticing a beautiful sunset, taking off your shoes to feel the earth supporting you, or taking a walk in nature. It may mean becoming an activist or advocate for the preservation and regeneration of the earth. Exploring this pathway will help you connect more intimately with the natural world that is our home.

The Global Community

Today we are connected globally like never before in terms of technology, trade, and travel. Ways to cultivate meaningful global connections and global thriving begin within each of our hearts as we realize our common humanity. A more peaceful world is possible as we begin to expand our consciousness to include concerns that are more global. There are many ways to cultivate global connections, including contributions to global and humanitarian causes, accepting and embracing the differences of persons from other cultures, and traveling to other countries to explore and discover new cultures. These threads of diversity weave a rich and beautiful tapestry. Along this pathway, you'll discover practical tips and ideas for connecting to the greater world.

Characteristics of a Thriving Community

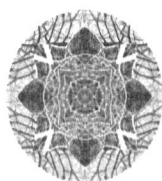 WHAT CONSTITUTES A THRIVING COMMUNITY? What are the primary hallmarks of strong communities? The following core characteristics are commonly found in healthy, balanced, and thriving communities, where individuals and groups connected to the community benefit through their participation in and engagement with the community at large. These characteristics are naturally supported by your deeper connection along The Spiral Path of Connection. They are found wherever we come together to experience True Community.

Connection and Community

People feel connected through shared values and goals that serve as a firm foundation for the community. These connections foster a deep sense of belonging and meaning for the members.

Wholeness and Integration

The community is seen and celebrated as an integrated whole, made up of individuals who themselves are connected with their inner truth and who are in holistic relationships with others in the community. The individuals and their relationships are beautiful threads in the rich and colorful tapestry of the community.

Action, Expansion, Engagement

Living and working together toward shared goals inspires actions that serve the greater good. Inspired action expands opportunities for all members to become engaged in meaningful activities that enrich the lives of all.

Truth and Alignment

The strong bonds of community are based in honesty and integrity that foster a sense of trust among the members. People in the community live in alignment with their own inner truth. Participants are clear about unique personal values that guide their interactions with others.

Nature and Natural Systems

People live in harmony with nature and honor the interconnectedness of all creation. They see themselves as part of nature, not separate from it. They hold nature as sacred and revered. Their actions serve to protect and preserve the natural environment for future generations.

Peace and Compassion

People in the community live peaceful, harmonious lives and enjoy the fullness that life in the community offers. Peace begins within. Compassion for others expands as each person re-connects with their inner truth of peace and harmony.

Sustainability

Community members are grateful for the abundance they enjoy. They make thoughtful choices about what they consume and how they spend their time and resources. They honor the earth and tread lightly upon it, using resources wisely and responsibly so that future generations may thrive.

Inclusivity

Every member is a valued contributor to the community. People's differences are valued and respected, and this diversity enriches the community rather than divides it.

Introduction: **Wholly Connected**

THIS IS A BOOK ABOUT CONNECTION. It is about living a connected life in a world that seems all too disconnected. At its heart, *Wholly Connected* holds the vision of coming together in community and thriving in a more compassionate and beautiful world. The book will explore the hallmarks of community. Yet it is also a guidebook filled with simple suggestions and practical steps you can take to live a more meaningful, fulfilled life. We will explore a myriad of ways you can enter into and thrive in the heart of community.

This book was born of a deep personal longing to make a difference in the world, to live a life with meaning and purpose in support of and in service to a more peaceful, compassionate, and connected world. Most importantly, this book is a response to the symptoms of disconnection so apparent in the world today. Together, we will explore practical pathways for a return to True Community, beginning with a deep connection to the True Self. Along five pathways emanating from The Spiral Path of Connection, we will encounter new ways to experience ourselves as whole and also as wholly connected.

Our Vital Need for Connection

Facilitating more meaningful connections to community has never been more important. Even with our seeming connectedness through technology, transportation, and global trade, there is a distinct feeling of disconnection from the ways that bring the most meaning to our lives. This disconnection affects all age groups, from teens to senior citizens, from children to those facing midlife challenges and transitions.

For example, while most teens in the US today are connected by social media, we see social media too often being used for less than positive purposes, such as cyber-bullying and trolling. At the other end of the age spectrum, many people who are a part of the growing population of senior citizens frequently live in isolation and loneliness. We hear news reports of rising rates of depression and suicide, of environmental disasters, of families affected by war and famine—all of which are related to disconnection from self and from community.

Many busy adults have become habituated to thinking and acting from the needs and desires of the ego. In a world where fierce independence and competition are valued and seen as the way to really get ahead, we are often led by the outer drive to success rather than the inner call to connection. The consequences of this approach often show up in the form of stress-related health problems, the experience of meaninglessness, or an overall lack of purpose.

At the same time, from busy moms to corporate executives and spanning across the age spectrum and all economic sectors, a sense of community and belonging is often cited as a key ingredient to thriving. The need for connection is critical. Connected communities are a vital component of a thriving society. More than ever we need to come together to understand and co-create solutions to the complex problems we are facing in our world today. No matter the presenting symptoms, almost always the root cause of issues in communities local and global is a felt sense of disconnection and lack of real meaning in life.

Practical Pathways

This book is intended as a personal guide for connection that is both inspiring and practical. It is written from the heart—a heart that knows the pain of feeling disconnected, separate, and lonely and a heart that also knows the immense joy that connection brings. It is a book that springs from a personal longing to feel connected, to really matter, to make a difference, and to express fully in the world. And it is a book that points the way to the realization of wholeness.

By walking The Spiral Path, we create stronger connections to community one person at a time. Our backdrop for our journey together is the mythical hero's journey, a journey we each must take to come home to ourselves. The way home is simple, but rarely easy. It is a way that is ever unfolding and unfurling, spiraling out from center of who we really are. The way is not ours to know in advance. This is the beauty and the mystery of the journey.

This book is a personal and practical guide to conscious living in community. It is meant to be read and experienced. To read it and then put it away on your bookshelf defeats its purpose. It is best read with a natural sense of curiosity and openness of heart. Return to the practices and connections exercises whenever you find yourself seeking a deeper connection along one of the five pathways to True Community.

You may not agree with everything in the book. Know that *Wholly Connected* is a book about your unique human experience as one that is integral to thriving communities and the world around you. As such, it is offered with the hope and expectation that its heart wisdom will resonate in ways that will inspire you to deeper exploration and connection to yourself and the world you live in. This book is written not from any sense of expertise, patronizing, or judgment. Rather, it is written from the lived experience of learning through pain, trial and error, and a commitment to tapping into the inner wisdom that is available to each of us. I invite you into that same experience of accepting what is and embracing all that is not known.

Perhaps one of the greatest lessons of life is coming to understand that we exist in not knowing. It is not ours to know. The invitation to each of us is that we come to an acceptance of our not knowing and live in the mystery of that state with a sense of awe, wonder, and gratitude. Eventually, we come to know that we are all in this life experience together, interconnected in ways we do not yet understand fully.

You are free to choose how you live and the ways in which you experience the world. The best place to start is right where you are. The way opens before you. It is up to you to take the next step to deeper self-understanding. Empowered to express your truth with authenticity and courage, you can join with others to co-create a more beautiful world.

Individual Wholeness, Webs of Connection

In our world everything is connected at some level, and so it is not possible to separate life into static and discrete parts. We all exist in webs of relationship. We are all inter-connected, living in a state of inter-BEing. We are interdependent, meant to be in relationship to one another, often through our connection to aligned communities.

The analogy of the human body as a system may be applied to any aspect of the natural world. It can also be applied to communities themselves. Systems are not discrete entities. Instead, they are connected in subtle ways to all other systems. Just as our bodies are made of many systems that work together to maintain our life existence, so it is in the larger world.

These systems are self-organizing and work together to maintain the integrity and balance of the whole. When one part of a system breaks down, the entire system is affected. Likewise, what affects one part is experienced within the whole system. The result of disruption in one area or part may be disease created by a persistent dis-ease that spreads to other parts or even the death of the entire system.

In healthy systems, wholeness is emanated from and reflected by all. When members of a community or parts of a greater system are balanced and centered on well-being, the whole system and individuals within it thrive and flourish. The field of quantum physics is now confirming our long-held inner wisdom that we are all connected in ways that we currently cannot fully grasp with our minds. We live in an incredible world of mystery, paradox, and possibility that can best be known through the experiencing of it rather than through attempts to understand it from a logical and rational perspective.

Wholeness implies movement and dynamic relationships. This book invites you to begin from your innermost self out and enter into the ever-expanding experience of life. Your journey begins with remembering the True Self and connecting more deeply with that. As your relationship with that wise self that resides at your true center strengthens, you will begin to trust yourself to open to a fuller experience of life by making deeper and more meaningful connections with the world around you. These connections include family and close relationships, the larger community, nature, and greater connection to the global community.

Connection fosters meaning and purpose in life. As you travel along The Spiral Path of Connection, you come to realize that you are always connected. You begin to see that you have never been separate except in your own mind's limited perspective. Your life journey inevitably leads you back to your home and to the True Self that, in truth, you never left. It has been there all along, waiting for you.

At times your journey may feel like a dark night of the soul. Rather than avoid the darkness you encounter along the way, walk through it. Experiencing it fully will help you remember the light. You can integrate darkness and light, coming into the full realization of your innate wholeness. Hearts broken open through suffering can allow in the light. Let any challenges along the way lead you back to your innate ability to expand into a greater experience of life.

Deep inner wisdom emerges through brokenness and pain. If we allow it, it will lead us back to deeper self-awareness and self-compassion. These gifts help us to better understand ourselves and then, in time, to reach out to others and to the world in which we live and interact. Suffering awakens a deep desire to serve others. If you are willing to embrace your innate wholeness, imperfections and all, and find your unique expression of that wholeness in the world around you, you will contribute to the co-creation of a more beautiful and compassionate world.

Awareness and Authenticity

Your journey to greater connection and community is best begun with a sense of curiosity, awe, and wonder. Such qualities draw you out and allow you to fulfill your innate longing to express yourself fully in the world in each present moment with greater ease and grace. In the process, you learn much more about yourself than you might otherwise have learned, because you have broadened your perspective. A deepening self-awareness stokes the flame of your desire to experience more. You will find a growing desire to feel more connected and alive.

In this way, you open your heart to embrace the whole world. Your perspective shifts and you see the connections and pathways to community more clearly. You understand how your connection to your True Self leads you into a fuller experience in other areas of your life.

We grow and open to greater connection naturally in the same way all things in nature grow organically. If you ignore this natural process of unfolding, you may live out your life in a state of apathy, sadness, loneliness, and despair, never experiencing the joy and fulfillment that true connection can bring. When you close your heart or shut off your conscious awareness to your own experience, you miss out on the beauty and mystery of the journey. It is your awareness of the growth process that makes it real for you and sparks your aliveness.

Likewise, full awareness fuels curiosity and wonder. As humans we naturally want to learn more about ourselves and the world around us. We long to feel fully connected, for we know innately that we are one with our world. Curiosity and wonder are natural states that are enhanced as we honor our inner longing for deeper, truer connection.

On your journey of expanding self-awareness, you also come to realize a deeper sense of authenticity. You begin to see more of who you really are. You naturally embrace wholeness and oneness, beginning within with your connection to you. This process leads to stronger outer connections that are at the very heart of building True Community.

There is a strong link between finding your true center and thriving in community. The outer world that you experience in community with others begins within. As we begin our journey together, become aware of your connection to your true center. How strong is your connection to your True Self? How connected do you feel as you move through life? To what degree do you currently experience authenticity and wholeness in your daily experience? Your answers to these questions provide key insights as we begin our journey of connection along The Spiral Path of Connection.

Connected Communities

This is a book that supports the co-creation of compassionate communities for a more peaceful world. It draws upon the universal human experience that plays out in the larger world. Thriving communities are connected communities. These communities begin within each one of us, and there is a strong connection between inner wholeness and thriving communities. Communities are born of and nurtured through connection, and we come to trust ourselves and others through our relationships in community. These connections are built one person at a time, one experience at a time. Together they make for strong and resilient communities that can withstand challenges that may arise.

Our collective story begins within each heart, within *your* heart. The story begins with your relationship to your authentic self. It must begin there, for you see the world through the lens of your unique and magnificent self. While the pathways along The Spiral Path of Connection point the way to the promise of a more beautiful world for all, change happens one person at a time. Individual choice will determine our success. What will your contribution be?

Self-love cultivates self-compassion that extends outward. Your deeper connection with your self opens your heart to greater awareness of your place in the world. In this state of loving awareness you see the world as an extension of yourself. With this perspective of connection you can celebrate your common humanity with others and begin to view the natural world around you as precious and sacred.

Connected communities are places of authenticity and belonging, where members are valued for their unique contribution to the whole. The experience of community begins with an honoring of all participants in the community, so that every member of the community has the opportunity to be wholly connected. Let's explore the five pathways for a return to True Community together.

1
The True Self
Pathways to Connection

Walk to the well.
Turn as the earth and the moon turn,
circling what they love. Whatever circles
comes from the center.

Rumi

Remembering Who You Are

THE SPIRAL PATH OF CONNECTION reminds us that life is a dynamic and organic process of ever-expanding unfurling from center. The five connection pathways we will explore invite us into a deepening sense of community and belonging. The first of those pathways leads to a deeper connection to your authentic self. We will call this the True Self.

Connection to the True Self is the central connection from which all other connections spring. As you remember who you are and reconnect with your true self, you open the way to greater connection to the world you live in. This deeper exploration of who you really are at your true center is what reconnects you to the very essence of your being.

On this journey of self-discovery, you are always unfolding to new depths of your truth. At the same time you are *enfolding*, including all things as you come to realize your expanding wholeness. The deeper you go, the more you discover about your true nature and what it means to be in True Community.

Start Where You Are

The best place to begin the pathway of connecting to the True Self is where you are in this moment. There is no need to worry about preparation for your journey. It begins right here, right where you are. You are already equipped with everything you need. Start where you are.

You hold unbelievable inner resources that you may draw upon at any time. These natural resources will guide and strengthen you on your pathway home to yourself. They have been yours all along. You only need to rediscover them. You have simply forgotten that your True Self is your sacred self. It is the center of who you really are, full of wonder and mystery. It is there for you in every moment of every day.

The True Self and the Ego Self

For the purposes of this book, "self" refers to *all* the aspects of what makes you "you." These aspects include the body, mind, emotions, and spirit. We each have a physical body, a mental body, an emotional body, and a spiritual body. What makes you who you are is the unique combination of your deep inner truth (your True Self), your personality, your temperament, and your life experiences. All of these working together are what make you the "you" that lives in the day-to-day world.

The True Self is your deepest inner self that connects you with all of humanity. It is who you are at your deepest, most authentic level. The True Self is that aspect of you that some refer to as Higher Self, Soul, God, or Source. It exists outside the confines of time, space, and the body; yet, it expresses through your body here in the world of form. When you are connected to your True Self, you are able to express in the world as uniquely you.

> When it comes to cultivating community, the place to start is with your true center and the heart of who you are.

The vastness of your True Self can transcend any and all physical limitations. Your True Self is pure wisdom. It is that aspect of you that serves as a witness to the ego self, which is associated with the mind and body. Your ego self is more concerned with the material world. The ego self refers to how you often show up in the world. Its focus is on the smaller you—the one tied to everyday roles and activities.

The ego's main concern is maintaining control of your everyday life and the way you move through the world. It has a narrow focus and sees life in terms of duality and separation. The ego self sees things in terms of "me and mine," but the True Self views things in terms of relationship and connection. The ego self is reactive and responds to changing emotions while the True Self is stable. When you listen to the ego self, you often find your mind in conflict and turmoil. But when you listen to the True Self, you experience peace.

The small ego self operates solely from the mind. It limits your perspective on who you are and what is possible for you. It allows you to see, but with a much narrower perspective than the expansive vision of the True Self. Despite its limitations, the ego self is not to be discarded. Its wisdom is needed. The ego provides useful information that helps you navigate your life. Remaining grounded in the physical world of day-to-day living is important, and the ego supports us in this way.

All the parts of you are needed to make your unique and vital contribution through a true expression of your wholeness. You simply need to come to a deeper awareness and acceptance of your wholeness. When you realize your wholeness, you accept and honor all the facets of who you are. You allow yourself to be guided by the deep wisdom of your True Self rather than being in the grips of the reactive and doubting ego self. The ego self compares, judges, and limits. The True Self understands the needs of the ego but is not controlled by it.

The True Self is the deeper self, which is connected to a level of consciousness that is peaceful, clear, and secure as well as creative, expansive, and wise. When you are living from the True Self, you experience greater clarity. You make better choices. As you are connected and centered in the True Self, solutions to problems arise from the deep wisdom that is a part of the essence of your wholeness.

While recognizing and honoring all aspects or facets of the self, the first three chapters of this book will focus most closely on that aspect that we call the True Self. Bringing your focus to your True

Self is not meant to diminish the importance of any of the other aspects of self. It is important to integrate all aspects of the self, and every facet of who you are is included in the remembrance of wholeness. As you bring the ego self and the True Self into greater balance and harmony, you unlock one key to connection and True Community.

Integration as a Key to Community

In order to experience wholeness, the process of integration is essential. Integration is about healing. It is also about exploring, accepting, and embracing all of the facets of who you are—to include those seen and those not seen. It is about going deeper within to uncover and rediscover aspects of yourself that you may have denied or ignored. Lastly, it is about the wonder and awe you experience when you realize your truth.

It is only when you feel a sense of wholeness and integration within that you are able to express love and compassion to others and fully engage with the world around you. Only when you feel whole and complete are you able to enter into and experience community. The place to start, when it comes to cultivating community is with your true center and the heart of who you are. True Community begins with our willingness to be in relationship with who we really are at the deepest level.

The pathway to connection with your True Self leads you to a deeper appreciation for all the aspects that make you who you are. As you explore deeper within, you realize that you are not perfect in your earthly body and your present life. Furthermore, you begin to know that is okay and come to realize that you are fine just as you are. You see that you are a uniquely magnificent person, as are all others. When you see yourself as anything less than this, you have simply forgotten the truth of who you really are.

The True Self has an innate capacity to include and embrace all aspects of your being that come together to make you who you are and inform your unique expression in the world. The True Self understands the role of the ego self. Because of this understanding, the True Self embraces the ego but is not controlled by it.

The True Self expresses from the center of truth that resides within you. It is solid in its wisdom. As you connect more deeply with the truth of who you are, you naturally align with those experiences that are right for you. You learn to let go. You allow yourself to be guided by your True Self.

A Desire to Know the True Self

As humans, we innately hold a curiosity about who we really are. That natural curiosity arises from an inner knowing of our truth—a knowing that our limited minds have often hidden away from us. Your pathway to inner connection begins with a desire to learn more about what makes you who you really are. As you connect, you want to go deeper and deeper on the journey of self-awareness. And the deeper your experience of your True Self, the more you yearn for even deeper connection.

What is the origin of this innate desire? If it is innate, then it must have been a part of us since the beginning. Some describe this desire as the essential longing to reconnect to our sacred Source or the energy of love that holds the world in balance as a self-regulating system. Some see this desire as the original desire to return to the "Beloved" (God). Whatever its origin, some never rekindle this inner flame of curiosity. This is often the result for those who do not welcome or appreciate the mystery of life. Instead, these individuals may choose to live out their lives in apathy, disconnection, and disinterest or wallow in sadness, despair, and loneliness.

Others simply ignore this inner desire to know one's self. As such, they may experience a sense of emptiness that they do not understand. Even so, they feel it always there. It is like an itch so deep it cannot be scratched. Seeking some kind of fulfillment, they may look outside of themselves to satisfy their deep, unnamable longing. Some seek fulfillment by accumulating more and more things. Outside distractions that perpetuate a lack of commitment to knowing the self may take the form of addictions to alcohol and other substances or activities such as gambling, sex, or shopping.

All of these are attempts to ignore or numb a deeper desire that is not recognized or understood. At the same time, these persons who push away their inner desire for connection within often experience an emptiness or hole in the soul. They are seeking connection and fulfillment through material substitutions for what is real. Yet, there are no material substitutions that can offer lasting fulfillment and satisfaction. Only daring to make the inner journey will quench the thirst for life.

The Taste of True Connection

To know that taste of true connection is unlike any other substitute. Material things and possessions offer only temporary fulfillment. The closer a thing is to original, the more lasting its innate value and the greater its fulfillment of that deeper desire. The further from Source one goes for the experience of the real and genuine, the less the lasting value to your fulfillment.

For example, handcrafted items created with loving hands are imbued with the energy of gratitude and appreciation from their creators. On the contrary, cheap goods manufactured by forced labor hold little or no radiance. This is because they do not come from love but rather are created from the greed of those who abuse and degrade a vulnerable population whom they coerce, manipulate, and use to produce these items for mass consumption.

Similarly, inspired writings are lasting. They arise from within the hearts of those who enjoy a close connection with the True Self. Sacred texts and original works of great art are imbued with the energy that flows from Source through the creators of such works. Because of this, their innate value can be felt and experienced. When you come closer to that which touches what is most authentic, your gifts become radiant and you have a more lasting impact on the world around you.

What Gives Meaning to My Life?

Understanding what you truly value points the way to the True Self and supports your quest for True Community. By asking what it is that is truly important to you and understanding what gives meaning to your life you gain a better understanding of who you really are. This supports greater connection to community.

It is equally important to understand how you interact in the world. A good place to start is with your values. Clarifying what you value most in life can help you identify the natural ways you connect with others. It can help you bridge the gap to community. As you identify what gives meaning to your life, you build new connections to community.

Individual values provide a good indication of your current level of self-awareness. Your values influence and determine how you make choices in life. Being able to identify your values goes a long way toward helping you better understand how you interact with others. When you know your values and live in a way that honors them, you are able to live a life of authenticity—one that is aligned with what is most important for you. To explore and clarify your values, ask yourself the following:

- *What is important to me?*
- *What gives meaning to my life?*
- *What do I really need or desire?*
- *What do I love to do?*

As you ask yourself these questions, notice what feelings come up. Do you notice an energy shift? Does your heart skip a beat? Such physical and emotional sensations help you understand and identify what resonates within you. Your feelings help you to better understand what sparks that natural curiosity, desire, and awe that connect you with your True Self.

Knowing your values can also help you make better choices in your day-to-day life. When you make choices that are in alignment with your values, you live a more authentic life. Because you are choosing based on what matters deep within and is most connected to who you really are, you experience greater flow and ease.

Knowing your values is a first step to understanding more deeply what gives your life meaning or purpose. At the same time, it is important to know that values are not carved in stone. Your values can change over time. As your self-awareness deepens, you may notice that your values shift and change to reflect your deeper understanding of yourself. As you become more intimately acquainted with your True Self, you grow in self-love and self-acceptance. This, in turn, leads to growth and expansion and affects what you value most.

A Love Affair with You

Connection with your True Self is similar to having a love affair —with yourself! Just as in our relationships with others, it can be easy to become complacent and to allow your relationship with your True Self to wither, lose its vitality, and eventually die. Your relationship with you must be cultivated and nurtured just as any relationship between two people.

For many people, giving and receiving love is very difficult to begin with. The idea of loving oneself may prove even more difficult where social norms value putting others before one's self. If you grew up in a family in which you did not feel loved or accepted or where you felt that you did not matter, you may struggle to love others and struggle even more to love yourself. It is not that you do not have the capacity for love. Instead, your life experiences have caused you to close your heart to receiving and giving love.

Others may have experienced being loved by their parents and by others outside the family. To these individuals, the practice of self-love comes more easily. If you have encountered blocks to giving and receiving love to any degree, your process of reconnection to your True Self may need to include deep personal work with a trained professional. A counselor or therapist can offer support as you come to greater realization of your wholeness.

In order for any relationship—even your relationship with your True Self—to endure, it must be based on the trust that unconditional love nurtures. In order to be able to receive love, we must feel that we are held in a safe and spacious space that allows for the free flow of love. The True Self resides in that spaciousness. There, you experience safety and room to grow.

Love is our natural state. We are ever held in love, and the True Self is made of love. It exists within a universal energy that holds all things in its deep embrace. Yet, we forget this pure state of existing in love as we live out our lives in the world of duality. It is being held in unconditional love that is at the root of what we all seek to remember.

The desire to return to wholeness is what often prompts the search for the True Self and a return to love. Your work now is to remember that you are precious and lovable. Your first step is to remember that you *are* Love. Loving yourself means loving the whole you—blemishes, inner wounds, and all. Loving yourself as you are begins with self-acceptance, self-forgiveness, and self-compassion.

Does the idea of self-love sound selfish to you? Some people feel very uncomfortable at the thought of what seems like putting self above others. Yet, it is impossible to love others if you cannot love yourself. Of course, there are situations in which we must take care of others and put them first. Babies, small children, and those who cannot care for themselves depend on others for their care. Their needs must be met, and we lovingly provide that care even as we remember to care for ourselves.

To love others is to give of ourselves from a deep inner reservoir of love than never dries up. Such universal love bonds us all together. It is enriched and expanded by our choice to embrace a path of loving the True Self.

The Practice of Self-Love

As you come to know and rediscover your True Self, you will see that there is much more to you than you ever realized. You are uniquely radiant, magnificent, and precious. When you adopt the practice of self-love, you naturally expand the love you have to give to others. It is easy to say, "I love myself." However, actually practicing self-love requires more than words.

Practicing self-love allows you to go deeper. It begins with you fully accepting who you are. Loving yourself is also linked to the choice to be kind to yourself. When you love yourself, you treat yourself with self-compassion and tender loving care.

With practice you will see that it becomes easier to allow yourself to be nurtured and loved and to nurture and love others. You will open up and allow the flow of love from the inner self into the whole of your life. Then, in time, you will begin to allow that love to expand outward into the world.

Here are some of the ways you can deepen the experience of extending love to yourself:

- ✓ **Self-Acceptance.** Love of self begins with self-acceptance. This means accepting yourself as you are right now, flaws and all. In order to love yourself, you have to intentionally choose love. Make the conscious choice to be loving and to allow yourself to be vulnerable enough to receive love.

- ✓ **Forgiveness.** Forgiveness for self has to do with letting go of your judgments about yourself. We all make mistakes, and we are here on earth to learn and grow. Instead of beating yourself up for mistakes you make, realize that no one is perfect. Choose to learn from your mistakes. Ask yourself, "What is the lesson this experience holds for me?" As your awareness deepens, you can rest in the knowing that there is really nothing to forgive. All is as it should be, whole and complete in itself and fully enfolded in the wholeness of all being. Cultivate self-compassion. Accept and let go. Surrender to the great unfolding. Gratitude for the journey will lead you home to yourself.

- ✓ **Allowing.** Allowing is a release of the compulsive need to "fix" everything. Let go of your perceived need to control outcomes for yourself or for others. When you can lean into life, to include the suffering you experience in your own life, you come to deeper understanding and acceptance of all life. Surrender to what is.

- ✓ **Feelings Awareness.** Become more aware of what you are feeling by consciously naming your feelings. Doing so will increase your self-awareness and self-compassion. Ask yourself, "What am I feeling right now in this moment?" Some people have grown up denying or repressing their feelings, because they were taught that certain feelings are bad or inappropriate. In order to gain deeper understanding of yourself and others, it is important that you become aware of the full range of human emotion. All feelings are okay. It is natural for feelings to surface and subside. Accepting your feelings as real is validating. Such a choice affirms your humanity and supports your connection to True Community.

✓ **Self-Development.** Your self-awareness expands as you allow yourself to go deeper within and learn more and more about who you are. Taking self-development courses, reading books on spiritual growth, and listening to inspirational speakers are all concrete ways to expand your learning and understanding. Cultivating a regular practice for personal development provides grounding and discipline for your inner journey. Commit to a path of self-growth.

✓ **Lightening Up.** Humor and laughter are stress releasers and offer effective ways to interrupt the habit of self-judgment and self-criticism. Take time to engage in childlike playfulness. Have fun!

✓ **Practicing Presence.** Practice being in the present moment. Rather than ruminating on the past or worrying about the future, notice what is happening right now. This practice gives your body a break from a habitual state of tension that you may have developed.

✓ **Gratitude.** An attitude of gratitude changes your perspective. Instead of focusing on all the things that are wrong or negative in your life, take the time to consider all for which you are grateful. The practice of gratitude has been proven to enhance well-being and happiness. It can open our hearts to appreciate good in the world. There are many specific practices that help us to cultivate gratitude in our lives. Some simple gratitude practices are included in a later chapter.

✓ **Love and Peace.** As you make the conscious choice to tap into and live from a place of love, it becomes natural for that love to flow outward to others. Then, that love is returned to you. Remember the line from the Prayer of St. Francis of Assisi: "For it is in giving that we receive." Love is a natural flow of giving and receiving. As you tap into your own inner peace and love, you express yourself in a more loving and peaceful way. World peace begins one heart at a time. Choose love. Choose peace.

✓ **Understanding Your Needs.** We all have needs. Some examples of universal needs include a need for expression, harmony, autonomy, integrity, community, contribution, connection, play, meaning, and well-being. Recognizing and responding to your specific needs is an important aspect of self-awareness and self-discovery. When you can identify what you need in any given situation and learn to communicate those needs to others, you experience life in fuller and more satisfying ways.

As you learn more about your own needs, it becomes easier for you to identify what others may need in any given situation. When you gain this insight, your interactions with others naturally become more compassionate. As you communicate your own needs and better understand the needs of others, you deepen your inner connection to yourself and strengthen the bonds of your relationships with others. As you gain deeper understanding of your needs, which are closely related to your values, you will also come to more clarity about what matters most to you. Take the time to discern what you most need and desire in your life.

- ✓ **Self-Compassion.** Self-compassion leads to the expression of kindness to yourself. Begin to treat yourself with tenderness rather than being critical and judgmental when you fail to meet your own expectations of yourself. Accept your imperfections, and begin with the awareness that we are all imperfect. Whenever possible, bring your awareness to your own humanity. As you cultivate self-compassion you can frame your experiences in this broader context of our shared humanity. Choose to recognize and feel a connection to others rather than remaining isolated in your suffering. You can cultivate self-compassion by becoming more mindful. Mindfulness allows you to be with what is and accept what is in the moment. If you are suffering, be with your pain. Acknowledge it and make choices from a place of mindfulness and compassion for yourself.

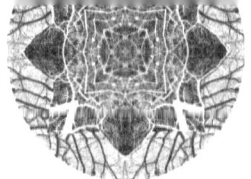

> I am so small I can barely be seen.
> How can this great love be inside me?
> Look at your eyes. They are so small,
> but they see enormous things.
>
> Rumi

Going Deeper: Seeing with New Eyes

THE JOURNEY ALONG THE SPIRAL PATH to your inner truth is one that takes you into even deeper understanding of who you really are. You begin to realize that you are seeing things differently and this new perspective opens you up to experiencing your world in a more expansive way. Deeply connected with your authentic self, you naturally want to live fully in expression of your truth. Following the wise guidance of your inner truth, your actions in the world arise from love and discernment. Now you seek periods of solitude and silence that reconnect you with the mystery that is life.

Focus Questions: *The True Self*

Reflect on the following focus questions to return to the experience of True Community through your connection to your True Self. In your journal, write down your responses to the following three questions:

1. At this point in my life, how would I describe my connection to my True Self?
2. How committed am I to going deeper on my pathway to connection with my True Self?
3. Connection with the True Self begins with self-love. How would I assess the love I have for myself right now?

Change Your Mindset, Change Your Life

A mindset is a set of beliefs or a mental construction that shapes your reality. Your mindset determines how you view the world you live in. Each person views life based on his or her beliefs. These beliefs have largely been shaped by your life experiences.

Here are some examples of mindsets:

- *The world is not safe.*
- *The world is beautiful and full of possibility.*
- *Money will make you happy.*
- *Money is the root of all evil.*
- *Everything happens for a reason.*
- *Stress is bad and harmful for you.*

Our mindsets are powerful because they affect how we think and act. Mindsets are like a lens that colors the way you experience life. For example, if you have the mindset that the world is not a safe place, you will be less likely to engage in the world due to your fears about your safety and well-being in it.

As you come to know and rediscover your True Self, you will see that there is much more to you than you ever realized! You will begin to notice that you are seeing yourself and the world with new eyes. You will have a new perspective on how you see the world, because you are now seeing with a new and expanded viewpoint. When you change your mindset, you change your life and open up new possibilities for True Community.

The Path of Expansion

Along the path to connection with the True Self, your heart is opening just as a flower blooms to the world. You develop the capacity to see beyond your small sense of self. Now, you can expand to consider new possibilities and new viewpoints for your life. Life becomes filled with possibilities that your small self never dreamed of. The world around you begins to look more beautiful. You are filled with hope for the future. Your heart opens in awe of all you now behold!

The ego self that has been in the driver's seat for so long no longer holds the power to limit your future by holding you small. It has been serving to protect you from hurt. It has worked hard to keep you safe from what it perceives as dangerous and threatening to you. It wants to hold you close in order to protect you from the danger and hurts of the outer world.

The ego's desperate grasp on you actually keeps you small. In such a state, you may fear taking risks. You may not be willing to open your heart to others outside your own "tribe" because you sense that they may pose a danger to you. Your ego self wants to keep you small so that you can feel that you are in control of what happens around you. This small self lives in fear of its own annihilation. It fears not being needed and so it enforces its will.

All these years, your smaller ego self has been on duty, holding you close and shading your eyes from the world beyond the small space it has seen as safe. Its hold is a desperate grasping and clinging. It is like a small, fearful child. Though it has served you well for its narrow purposes and it is an integral part of who you are, your ego is not all of who you really are.

Now you are ready to live life more expansively. Embrace the ego self as an aspect of your wholeness. Know that it serves a purpose. But see with new eyes that it is no longer in total control. It can now take a backseat so that you can allow your True Self to express wholeheartedly in the world. Now you will find that you can experience life in a more innocent, and playful way.

With this newly expanded vision and awareness, you recognize all aspects of you. You may now accept and embrace them all but no longer allow any one aspect to seize control or set your course. From here forward, you can choose to act in the world from your inner True Self—a self that empowers you to make wise choices and to live a fulfilling and meaningful life. Now you may inwardly bless your wholeness as you allow all the aspects of you to join in a harmonious chorus of being. With one voice, you can move forward with confidence.

Reclaim Your Voice of Truth

As you connect with your True Self, you can more easily see your own wholeness mirrored in the outer world of your experience. Your inner connection fosters a realization of connection with others, even as remembering your oneness with all opens the way for deeper connection in your individual life. While we are all connected to one another and share a common humanity, it is equally important to remember that each of us is unique.

There is no one else quite like you. You are uniquely magnificent and radiant in your truth. The radiant light of each one of us is needed for wholeness to be expressed fully in our world. In order to know ourselves deeply, we must tune in to the whole being of who we really are. This is why connection along this first pathway is so vitally important and your first priority as you seek a return to True Community.

When you connect with your True Self, you are open to accessing all of who you are. You remember your wholeness. You tap the wonder and magnificence of what makes you who you are. When you bring all facets of yourself into alignment, you reconnect to your voice of truth. Your desire to express your truth more fully in the world is awakened.

As your innate desire to connect comes alive, you begin to experience a desire to sing in full harmony with the whole world. You are ready to step up and out into the world in a way that you never thought possible. You are empowered from within.

As you connect more fully with your True Self, you naturally live in more authenticity and in greater alignment with your truth, because now you hold self-awareness of that inner truth. No more need to wander in desperate seeking. You have come home to yourself at last!

Being Versus Doing

The more you connect to your True Self, the more you yearn to express your truth in the world. There are limitless ways to do that, but some will resonate for you more than others. The key to expressing your voice in the world is to first distinguish between being and doing.

Many struggle throughout their lives, trying to resolve the age-old issue of being and doing. For example, many people feel compelled to do something and are then driven by a frantic compulsion for busyness that is often dictated by their perception of society's expectation of busyness. They move quickly into action so as to not be idle or "lazy." Some people learn to engage in busyness as a distraction that allows them to avoid looking within themselves, because they fear what they may discover about themselves.

In truth, you can only engage in meaningful doing through the awareness of who you really are. Doing without being is empty and wasted action. Doing through being your truth is right action in the world, fueled by the energy of love. So then your quandary may be about which specific actions you take in the world. You will discover that the what or the true purpose of your life arises from and is connected to your ability to be authentic.

Authentic expression is connected to what you value and arises from your core essence. Again, you may find it helpful to reflect on what gives your life meaning. Consider the following questions:

- What do I enjoy doing?
- What makes my heart sing?
- What are my talents and skills?
- What am I really good at?
- What activities do I lose myself in as I engage in them?
- What wisdom does my inner guidance have to offer to me about the things I love?

These questions can help you gain clarity on what is uniquely yours to be and do in the world. Being your truth in the world might mean that you express yourself gently as a loving mother, as a caregiver, or as a loving neighbor. When you are aligned with your inner self and operating from that truth, your actions naturally flow from that state of being in fullness. Being your truth in the world means expressing the essence of who you really are, no matter the actions involved in that expression. It is really a matter of your BEing in the world.

Love in Action

Actions that spring from our inner truth have inherently greater impact in the world. Far from representing action for action's sake, actions chosen with intent and based on a consideration of who you truly are and how you choose to use your voice of truth in the world are potent. Essentially, action taken from this place is infused with the transformative power of love.

Many of the world's wisdom traditions speak to aligned action. For example, the term "right action" comes from the Buddhist tradition's Noble Eightfold Path. In this tradition, right speech, right action, and right livelihood are associated with moral virtue. In truth, this understanding of correct action is more about what one does *not* do than it is about taking any particular action.

Love in action refers to actions that naturally arise from a desire to express your truth in the world as you connect more deeply with your True Self. This kind of action or *doing*, fueled by love and guided by your inner wisdom, is wise or discerned action that is aligned with your truth. Rather than being guided by reminders of what not to do, love in action feels right because it is constantly nudging us to seek a fuller and more expansive expression, ever opening us to new possibilities.

Likewise, action that arises from one's inner wisdom is much more than action for action's sake. Action that is informed by a choice for being over doing and activated by thoughtful choices to use one's voice of truth intentionally and with love is action at the highest level. Such action naturally flows from a strong connection to the True Self and the ability to connect to your intuition.

Trusting Your Inner Guidance

Connecting with your True Self opens up a whole new world of possibility for you. Suddenly, you realize that you have access to inner resources and tools for your life's journey—tools and resources that you never dared to imagine. And all of this is all available to you at any moment. You have access to unlimited resources of higher guidance. You have always had this access; but now, with your deepening awareness, you come to trust that there is much more to yourself than you ever imagined possible.

Tapping into your inner guidance may take many forms. Some people use prayer, contemplation, or meditation to get in touch with the True Self. Accessing your inner wisdom and asking for guidance may seem a stretch for you. Relax and allow yourself to be led to what is natural for you. Some call this inner guidance intuition, referring to the hunches, gut feelings, or flashes of inspiration that just seem to happen without any prior notice. We have all heard about trusting our intuition. The path to accessing that higher-level awareness is a simple and natural one. It is a matter of putting aside your rational mind, quieting your thoughts, and becoming still.

All that is required is an allowing for the natural shift to a higher level of consciousness. Begin with deep listening. Tune in to your inner wisdom. Practice patience as you open to hear "the still small voice within." Part of trusting your True Self involves a willingness to let go and leave room for what cannot be known.

Trusting the Mystery

Many people are so accustomed to relying on the rational mind that coming to trust higher levels of consciousness seems too mysterious a thing to hope for or believe. We have been conditioned to believe only in what we can experience through our physical senses of seeing, hearing, touching, tasting, and smelling. Most of us in the Western World have been conditioned to rely almost exclusively on the scientific method. Anything that cannot be tested scientifically is considered suspect.

Increasingly, scientific fields such as quantum physics and neurobiology are showing that there is much more to us and to our world than we ever thought possible. New ideas and new realities are opening before us. Our worldview is broadening to include vastly expanded possibilities. We can do the same as we connect to the inner experience of ourselves.

We live in a world of wonder and paradox, a world of mystery and possibility. With our expanded awareness of the world, it suddenly becomes more believable that we also have access to higher states of consciousness or a higher self. We can begin to connect to a greater capacity to access guidance from levels of awareness that far exceed the levels of everyday functioning to which we have become accustomed.

Over time, you will see that higher states of consciousness become more normal for you. You will begin to notice that you are moving into a state of greater trust and acceptance. That trust is strengthened and affirmed through your experience of it. Coming to trust your inner guidance is a process that deepens with practice and allowing. Allowing room for mystery, you open to new understanding and connection to life.

Sometimes that connection comes from unexpected places. It can even begin in the stillness and moments where it appears nothing is happening.

Silence and Solitude

As you explore ways to connect more meaningfully to your True Self and the world you live in, you may notice a newly heightened need for silence and solitude. Experiencing silence is essentially a return to the essence of our being. Silence reconnects us to that place from which form arose. Sitting in silence allows the chatter of our minds to settle. But rather than being only a place of emptiness, silent spaces are filled with the potentiality from which all form, including sound, arises.

The key to accessing silence is stillness. Find time to allow yourself to be still. Then you can enter that place of silence deep within and discover whole new worlds of possibility for yourself. These inner connections are vital components to making connections with others and experiencing True Community.

Solitude can be regenerative and refreshing. It allows us time for reflection and can unleash creative energies that have previously been blocked. Being in solitude is a powerful way to go deeper within. Many people discover, sometimes quite unexpectedly, that they thrive in solitude. They may choose to be alone for long periods of time.

Despite the common misconception to the contrary, solitude is not loneliness. There are distinct differences between solitude and loneliness. Loneliness is a negative state of mind characterized by feeling alone and isolated. In a state of loneliness, we feel disconnected from ourselves and others. It is possible to be lonely or to feel alone even when we are surrounded by people. While loneliness arises from perceived lack, solitude is a state of being home within one's self.

While solitude fosters more meaningful and deeper connections to the True Self and ultimately to the world, loneliness cuts us off from connecting with others. Knowing the difference between loneliness and solitude can deepen our own understanding and help us cultivate compassion. It can also inspire us to reach out to those who suffer from loneliness. Ultimately, solitude enhances connection and helps us develop a deeper awareness of our present state.

Mindfulness: BE-ing in the Present Moment

Mindfulness is the practice of being in the present moment. Being in the present means that our focus and attention is on what is happening within ourselves or around us as it is happening right now. Mindfulness is about allowing what is to be, without trying to change it or control it. We are simply living it, experiencing it for what it is, noticing it, and allowing it to arise.

The present moment exists beyond the flow of time as we typically experience time in our everyday lives. We may think about the past or fear the future, but these are only states of mind. Such thoughts represent the activity of the ego mind. Regret and worry are the go-to activities of the ego mind. We can only take action *right now*, in the present moment.

When we are in the present, it is impossible to think about the past or worry about the future. To be mindfully present is to be centered in the present moment. The present moment is really the only moment there is in which we can act. It is the only opening we have to take action in the world. As such, the present moment holds unlimited potential for us. We can think about taking action in the future or regret actions we took in the past, but we can only *do* in this now moment. This is why the present moment is the only moment from which we can tap into our true power.

Practices for Connection: The True Self

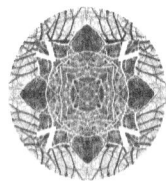

THIS CHAPTER OFFERS PRACTICES to ground you in the experience of your True Self. Refer to these practices and the questions for deeper reflection as you continue to strengthen your connection to your True Self in the coming months and years.

Experience Presence

Experiencing presence is a powerful practice that grounds you in the present moment. This practice, which greatly enhances a connection to your True Self, is often called mindfulness. When you bring your attention to the present moment, it is impossible to worry about the past or fear the future.

The present moment is timeless. It exists beyond and outside of time as we experience it in our linear way of recognizing and understanding time. As you practice being fully present, your awareness of time dissolves. Being the only moment that truly exists, it is from within the present moment that we must act. In truth, it is impossible to act in the past or in the future; the present moment is the only point of action. It is the only moment we have. Acting in the moment and from the guidance of our higher wisdom is right action from our wise and True Self.

Practicing presence is a helpful stress management tool. In the midst of a hectic life, it is easy to lose yourself in the busyness of life. Pausing to experience the present moment can allow you to recharge and reconnect. Being present quiets your mind chatter. It helps to clear a space for connecting with your inner self.

The intentional practice of presence helps to bring your awareness back to your True Self. Over time, self-connection becomes second nature. Here are a few simple ways to practice being fully present in the moment:

- ✓ **Experience the Five Senses.** Sit quietly in a comfortable position. Take in a few deep breaths, inhaling and exhaling fully. Notice the coolness of your breath as it enters your nostrils. Feel the warmth of your breath as you exhale. Now, return your breathing to its natural rhythm. As you breathe naturally, notice something you see. It can be anything. Just allow your eyes to come to rest on one object in your field of vision. Next, notice something that you hear. Listen for a few moments, bringing your full awareness to what you hear.

Next, notice the taste in your mouth. Simply notice. Now, notice something you feel on or in your body. It may be the feel of your shirt on your body. It may be a slight breeze that you feel on your skin. It may be the way the chair is supporting your back. Whatever you feel through the sensation of your skin, notice that. Finally, notice one thing you smell. This may be a pleasant aroma in the air or anything that you smell in the present moment. Sit for a few more minutes, breathing gently. Give thanks for your five senses and your ability to experience the world through them.

- ✓ **Notice Nature.** Consider this activity as you take a nature walk. Practice noticing nature anytime you are outdoors. Simply quiet your mind and begin to notice the natural world around you. Notice the colors of the leaves on the trees and the way the leaves move in the breeze. You might listen for birds singing or notice the way clouds drift in the sky. Spend as long as you want immersed in the experience of the natural world. The purpose of this activity is to bring you into the present moment. Take time daily to connect more deeply with the natural world of which you are an integral part.

- ✓ **Practice Gratitude.** There is a growing body of research on the benefits of practicing gratitude. Consciously practicing gratitude gets us in the habit of opening our hearts and really experiencing the energy of love flowing through us. It reminds us of what is good in the world. Gratitude is about being mindful of and appreciating people, places, and things that bring us joy and fulfillment. It is associated with well-being. Here are a few simple gratitude practices:

- Daily, upon awakening, think of three things you are grateful for and give thanks for them.
- Keep a gratitude journal in which you record people or things for which you are grateful.
- Practice gratitude meditations by bringing your awareness to something for which you are grateful.

✓ **Practice Regular Self-Care.** Consider a weekly date with yourself for self-care. Just knowing you will set aside time to tend to your physical, emotional, mental, and spiritual well-being is a step in the right direction! Treat yourself with tender loving care. Caring for yourself includes caring for your body. Take time to treat your body as a sacred vessel that grounds you in the physical world. Get proper rest, engage in physical activity, and invest in nourishing and nutritious foods. Nurture your body. Learn to listen to it. Your body is continually communicating its needs and is an important messenger for the deeper aspects of yourself.

✓ **Cultivate Self-Compassion.** Self-compassion is all about being kind to ourselves. It is also about treating ourselves with tenderness, rather than being critical and judgmental when we fail or do not meet our own expectations of ourselves. The next time you hear that voice in your head criticizing you for your latest mistake, turn the statement around into one that affirms your true self. Self-compassion invites us to accept our imperfections and come to the awareness that we are all imperfect. As we cultivate self-compassion we can frame our experiences in terms of our shared humanity. We begin to feel connected to our common humanity rather than isolated in our suffering. We also cultivate self-compassion by being more mindful and allowing ourselves to be with what is. If we are suffering, we can be with the pain, accepting what is in the moment, acknowledging our pain, and then making choices from a place of mindfulness and connection.

- ✓ **Adopt a Regular Connection Practice.** Whether it is meditation, yoga, journaling, or a similar activity of your choice, add a consistent daily or weekly practice to your routine. The discipline of a regular practice grounds you and offers a space for regular connection with yourself in deeper and more meaningful ways.

Tap into the Wisdom of Your Body

Your physical body is a portal to a deeper understanding and connection to your True Self. Tuning into your body takes practice and intention. It is easy to take the body for granted or to ignore its needs and the many messages it holds for you, but the body is an important aspect of your wholeness. In order to understand your whole self, it is necessary that you learn to listen to your body.

The body is the physical vessel for your being, and so it is sacred. It holds the True Self in a physical form and grounds us to the natural world. Our innate inner wisdom is expressed in the physical world through the body. What is your body telling you right now?

Here are some practices to tune into the wisdom of the body:

- ✓ **Noticing the Body.** Sit quietly, in a comfortable position. Take a few deep breaths. Breathe in deeply, then exhale fully. Repeat for 3 to 5 breaths. Then, let your breath return to its natural rhythm. Next, allow your mind to slowly scan your body, noticing any areas of tension or discomfort. The purpose of this exercise is not to specifically relax the body. Rather, this is an exercise intended to allow you to simply notice your body. As you notice any areas of tension or discomfort, consider the message of the pain or discomfort. What could your discomfort be telling you about yourself?

- ✓ **Free Movement or Dance.** This practice can be done alone or in a group. Free movement or dance allows the body to express through movement without the interference from your judging mind. This practice is enhanced when you move to music that inspires you. As you move, let go of the limitations of the rational mind and allow the body to move freely. In addition to relieving stress, this practice has other important health benefits. Simply getting up and moving can change the pace and put you in an expanded space of awareness.

- ✓ **Embodying Your True Power.** This activity is a kind of embodied visualization. To prepare for the activity, sit in a comfortable position with your spine erect but not rigid. Close your eyes or gently gaze downward. Take a few deep breaths, inhaling and exhaling fully. Allow any thoughts that arise to gently settle into the background. As you breathe, get in touch with the center of your being. How does your body feel as you connect with the power that arises from the inner truth of your being?

  Now, allow yourself to embody the power that arises within you. Really feel the flow of power inside your body. You may notice that you sit taller. You may feel a shift or notice an expansion from within. You may choose to stand up. Allow your body to assume a stance that is connected with your inner power. What does your power stance look like? How do you feel as you embody your inner power? Use this activity any time you feel disempowered or disconnected. Assuming your power stance can immediately serve as an anchor to your inner power and wisdom.

Intuitive Journaling Practice

Intuitive journaling is a satisfying experience of handwritten journaling that can lead to deeper self-understanding and self-awareness. The experience of putting pen to paper centers you in the present moment, allowing you to be completely immersed in the act of self-expression. Fully engaged in the moment, you bring your presence forward, allowing any judgments and the voice of your inner critic to fade into the background. Through this practice of intuitive journaling, you give voice to the unique truth that yearns for expression in and through your life.

This practice connects you to your True Self and helps you to reclaim your voice of truth. Being fully present in the moment, you engage body, mind, and spirit to tap into the creative flow and access the deeper wisdom that resides within you. Intuitive journaling gives you greater access to your unique inner voice—what some refer to as the True Self, the Heart, the Soul, the Wise Self, the Guide, or God.

By practicing this deep form of journaling you can learn how to recognize and trust the inner guidance that is always accessible to you. The practice is a form of dialogue between your ego self, a voice often driven by fear and existing in a state of confusion or conflict, and your True Self that exists in the light of truth, love, peace, and presence. Over time, your intuitive journal becomes a sacred record of your unfolding self-awareness and integration.

Steps for Intuitive Journaling Practice

1. Go to a quiet space away from distractions.
2. Choose a journal and writing instrument that you love.
3. Light a candle for centering and to symbolize your inner light of wisdom
4. Take a few deep breaths. Lean into and fully experience the present moment.
5. Write or say a mantra, prayer, or invitation to invoke the energy of your higher self. Enter into the space of sacred dialogue with your True Self.

6. Dialogue Part I: Allow the small ego self its full expression. Write from the voice of the ego. Allow this voice to empty itself onto the page. Pour out your thoughts, concerns, fears, and questions. Record your full experience, to include accompanying emotions and body sensations. Allow the ego self to acknowledge the presence of your higher self and express gratitude for being fully heard by your higher self.

7. Dialogue Part II: Allow your higher self its full expression in response to the ego self. Place your hand over your heart space, acknowledging and embracing the emptying. Express your gratitude for the vulnerability demonstrated by the ego self. Allow love to flow into the emptied space. Begin writing in response to the ego self, addressing this self in a loving, tender way. Allow the flow of love and inner wisdom to pour in to the emptiness. Avoid censoring or any interference from the rational mind. Avoid assigning words from the small mind's desires and expectations. Continue writing. This may feel unnatural and awkward at first, but allow your higher self to express until you feel complete.

8. In conclusion, add a written expression of gratitude from your ego self to your higher self for its message of guidance and wisdom. End with a signature written expression such as "And so it is." Or, "All is well."

9. Take a few deep breaths. Notice how you feel in the present moment.

21 Questions for Deeper Reflection

1. Who am I *really*?
2. What makes my heart sing?
3. What breaks my heart?
4. How do I practice self-care?
5. What am I hiding from others or denying to myself?
6. How am I expressing my True Self in the world?
7. What do I like about myself?
8. What is holding me back?
9. What is my vision for my life?
10. What is possible for me?
11. How can I bring more creativity, fun, and joy into my life?
12. What makes me laugh?
13. What do I need to say, "Yes!" to?
14. How am I hiding my radiant magnificence from the world?
15. What am I curious about?
16. What do I *really* need? What do I *really* want?
17. What is important to me? What are my values?
18. How is my life honoring my values?
19. How is my being in the world changing the world?
20. What do I love about myself?
21. What is uniquely mine to express in the world?

2

Family and Friends
Pathways to Connection

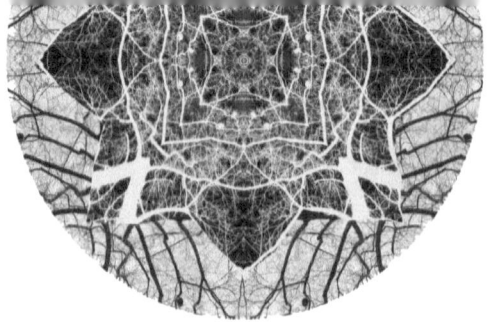

> Each friend represents a world in us, a world
> possibly not born until they arrive, and it is only by
> this meeting that a new world is born.
>
> Anais Nin

Close Connections and Community

AS WE CONTINUE TO EXPLORE the five connection pathways along The Spiral Path that leads us into a deepening sense of community and belonging, we come to the second point of connection to family and friends. Once you have established a deepening connection with your True Self, you begin to notice the ways you intentionally connect with the circle of people you encounter day by day. From here, we explore the close relationships that bring us into True Community.

These close relationships might include the family into which you were born as well as your spouse or significant other and children. It might also include your chosen family—those with whom you have developed a close bond through the years. Friends from your neighborhood, friends from your workplace, friends from church and other centers of community, and friends from social networks offline and online are also included in this category of close relationships.

The Space Between

Relationships take root, grow, and are nurtured in the space between two or more people, but they begin within each of us. Our ability to connect with others depends on our connection with our own True Self. Your close relationships with family and friends are extensions of your relationship with yourself. As you come to know and trust the truth of who you really are, it is easier for you to extend yourself to others.

For relationships to develop fully and thrive, they must be nurtured in an environment of trust and love. Think of your relationships like a garden that must be carefully tended and maintained in order for fulfilling relationships to take hold and fully blossom. Consider how you might create a space for your relationships with family and friends to flourish and grow.

If you were raised in a nurturing environment, you likely find that making meaningful connections with others comes much easier. Even if that is not the case, draw deeply on what you know about who you are as you connect with other individuals and groups. As you bring your True Self forward fully in your relationships with others, enjoying time together, discovering your commonalities, sharing values and a vision for tomorrow, you naturally cultivate the experience of community.

It is important to tend the whole garden so that the entire system is nurtured and flourishes. Because we are all connected, we must not overlook any aspect of the whole or the entire system will suffer. To connect to community, connect often and in meaningful ways with family and friends.

Your relationships with family and friends will afford you many opportunities to find meaningful expression in the world. These closest connections are a key to discovering new dimensions of True Community. The space between our lives and the lives of our closest friends and family members is a rich and fertile ground for learning more about who you are and about the natural connections that support and sustain your relationships with others. As you move through your days, value the space between, knowing it supports your full flourishing in relationship.

Cultivating Joyful Relationships

Connections with family and friends can bring us into the experience of great joy. These relationships help us connect to greater meaning and purpose in our lives. As satisfying as these relationships can be for us, they also can be complex and sometimes conflicted. Thriving and resilient relationships do not just happen; they must be cultivated and nurtured in loving and supportive environments.

Each of us bears a responsibility for the creation of True Community through our choice to tend to and nurture the quality of our relationships with ourselves and others. Take a quick inventory of how you are showing up in your closest relationships. Ask yourself these questions:

- How am I bringing my most authentic self to each of my relationships with family and friends?
- How do I choose to invest my time and attention in these important relationships?
- Am I cultivating a sense of safety and belonging, joy and compassion, trust and happiness within each of these primary relationships?
- How can I nurture strong and lasting relationships that support my full thriving in True Community?

Barriers To Community with Family and Friends

Cultivating community based on strong family and friend relationships requires conscious effort and commitment. Not everyone is ready and willing to make that effort or rise to the level of commitment that will lead to improved relationships with family and friends. In addition to a lack of willingness to make the required commitment to invest in relationships, the following are examples of common barriers to cultivating community by strengthening key relationships:

Time. Perhaps the greatest barrier to cultivating community through meaningful connections with family and friends is a perceived *lack of time*. We lead busy, hectic lives, and it does require persistence and patience to set aside quality time for family and friends. It's easy to overlook the importance of such connections and fall into a predictable pattern of saying we just don't have time. Questions to consider:

- How committed am I to cultivating True Community through connections with family and friends?
- Am I willing to invest time in cultivating the close bonds necessary for True Community?

Preferred Style. Some people prefer interacting in small group situations rather than larger circles. These individuals may believe that their preference for small group interaction precludes their contribution to cultivating True Community. Contrary to this common belief, a natural preference for quality over quantity in relationships actually adds a depth and richness to community.

How we connect with others is always a matter of choice. If you prefer small group connections, the key is to find simple ways to connect, both one-to-one and in small groups. Creating containers of protected time that is dedicated to such connections is one helpful practice. For example, many families and small groups enjoy planning fun events and outings on a regular basis.

Questions to consider:

- How do I consistently prioritize connections with family and friends?
- How do I prefer to connect with family and friends? Do I prefer small group settings, larger gatherings, or one-to-one connections?
- What is my level of commitment to bringing my True Self forward in my connections with others?

Deepening Awareness and Alignment

Our relationships with one another form within social systems that support and sustain the larger natural systems within our world. As our connections grow stronger, we are better equipped to weave the fabric of a more peaceful and harmonious community. The return to True Community is made possible by our choice to nurture and strengthen the bonds that connect us to others.

Living in alignment with our underlying values and expressing our True Self in the world helps others, to include family members and close friends, to see and feel our genuineness. It helps others know they can trust us on an ongoing basis. As we operate from our true nature more and more in our everyday relationships, we experience greater thriving. This, in turn, supports a deepening of community and benefits the greater good.

The gift of our closest relationships is a growing awareness, sometimes an uncomfortable one, that we are all connected in webs of interdependence. Our close relationships invite us to bring more of ourselves into conscious relationship with one another. The relationships we form within the tight-knit community of family and friends can serve as reminders of our oneness with and connection to the whole.

Our closest connections provide a nurturing space for us to learn about ourselves. Through relationships formed with friends and family, we deepen our awareness of who we are and how we fit into our world. As we experience the satisfying connections experienced within this first circle of external community we are reminded of our unity with others. Even when these close relationships present us with challenges, we gain a deeper understanding of ourselves and the imperative of remaining connected within and without.

12 Key Characteristics for Resilient Relationships

Relationships are as unique as the individuals who form them. Thriving relationships share key characteristics, which create the conditions for resilient relationships. Consider how and to what degree these core qualities are present in your closest connections. Take note of those which may be missing from your experience of community with your closest connections.

1. **Love.** Love is the basis of all human relationships. It connects one thing to another. All things are connected and held together in the energy of love. Many people think they have to seek lasting love. As such, they may spend a lifetime looking for the love that is already within their hearts! For positive, loving relationships to blossom and grow the only requirement is that you open your heart to the possibilities inherent in the coming together of two or more people. Relationships with family members and close friends provide many opportunities for you to experience the flow of giving and receiving love, and love flows most freely when hearts open to the full experience of love.

   How open are you to the fullest experience of love?

2. **Authenticity.** When you live from the wisdom of the True Self and align your actions with who you really are, authenticity is the natural and predictable result. When you are authentic in your relationships with others, you do not hide behind pretense or falsity. Instead, you have a deep inner knowing of who you really are and show up in relationships by expressing your truth.

   How are you showing up fully as your authentic self in your relationships with family and friends?

3. **Intrinsic Value.** As you experience the world through your connection with your True Self, you see the sacredness in all beings and things. You see that every living thing has intrinsic value because you understand that we have all come to express our BEing in the world. No one of us needs to do anything to earn value. We are all created equal. You have value simply because you *are*. When you come to this realization, your heart opens to embrace the world. The relationships that are born of your open-hearted willingness to be a part of the world and to meet others where they are add more value to the world and help create the conditions for True Community. Watch your world expand as you experience ever-deepening connections with those around you!

   How can you open yourself to embrace the intrinsic value of each of your family members and close friends?

4. **Sense of Safety.** We feel safest in relationships built on a solid foundation of love, support, authenticity, and openness. Our connections with family and friends thrive and grow when we feel secure and protected—even when we are confronted with threats of danger. When you feel safe in relation to yourself and others, you are more willing to open yourself to experience the world around you—to include connecting more closely with your family and friends. Rather than constricting yourself due to fear, you feel safe enough to lean in to life. You begin to open yourself to new experiences of friendship and connection. When you experience safety, you are more likely to take risks that can result in living larger in the world.

   How does your sense of safety allow you to form closer connections with family members and friends?

5. **Trust.** Trust grows in the held space of safety and security. As you begin to feel safe in your world and expand your life experiences, you come to realize that you are surrounded by people you can trust. Likewise, your cultivation of trust helps others to see that they can depend on you. A sense of trust deepens with each and every experience of being safe and secure in the field of love.

   How do you hold a safe and non-threatening space for others to be themselves in their relationships with you?

6. **Vulnerability.** When you feel held in the spaciousness of love and trust, you feel safe and secure enough to be yourself, imperfections and all. Rather than hide behind your fear of exposing your imperfections, you understand that no one is perfect. In deep relationship with another, you begin to feel safe enough to allow the other person to see all of who you really are. Such vulnerability requires trust. It requires the courage to show up as the real you in all relationships. In supportive connections with those you trust, you feel free to lean into life even as you open yourself to new experiences you may have previously avoided due to the fear of exposing your perceived imperfections. True Community can take root where we find the courage to embrace our whole selves and become vulnerable in relationship with one another.

   Who are the people in your circle of family and friends with whom you can be vulnerable?

7. **Compassion.** Compassion for others begins with compassion for self. You cultivate this core quality for resilient relationships through the acceptance of

who you are, by realizing your imperfections, and in knowing that no one of us is perfect. As your compassion for yourself grows, it will become more and more natural for you to open your heart and hands to help those around you.

How does accepting your own imperfections open you to accepting the imperfections of others?

8. **Presence.** Your connection with another is strengthened when you are fully present to them. Being fully present affirms their intrinsic worth. Your attentiveness in relationships helps others to feel seen and heard. It conveys to them that they really matter to you. Likewise, when others are fully present to you, you feel seen, heard, and valued.

   How do you feel when fully present with a close friend?

9. **Listening.** Listening is closely related to being fully present in your relationships. In full presence with each other, we open our hearts and listen deeply to what others say with their words as well as what they communicate non-verbally. Deep listening is about more than simply listening with your sense of hearing. It is also about noticing body language, facial expressions, and physical gestures. Attention to non-verbal communication can provide valuable cues about what the other person is feeling, needing, or trying to say. As you listen deeply, pay attention to periods of silence from the other person. Consciously holding space for silence in conversation and in relationship to one another can add richness to the overall interaction and help the other person feel affirmed. Silence delivers a powerful message!

How does your interaction with a family member or friend change when you listen deeply to what they are saying?

10. **Integrity.** Integrity infers a steadfast alignment between who you are and your outer actions. Being in integrity means that you do what you say you will do. Your integrity can be measured in part by your dependability. How dependable are you? Do you keep your word? Do you do what you promise to do? Can your children rely on you to be there when they need you? Dependability helps others to trust you and feel they can rely on you to do what you have said you will do.

    In your relationships with family members and friends, how reliable are you? Do you keep your word?

11. **Responsibility.** You are personally responsible for your own choices and actions. This awareness can be very empowering. Bringing that same sense of responsibility to the context of your relationships with others amplifies its effect. When you are in integrity and enter responsibly into relationship with others, your perspective expands. You see that in community you can discover common ground that embraces both the diversity and the commonalities of the group. Each participant in community has a personal responsibility to nurture and sustain the larger group and to see each person as a valued contributor to the whole. In the context of connections with others, being seen and feeling valued for your contributions to community can add another dimension of meaning and purpose to your life.

    What are your responsibilities in your close relationships?

12. **Acceptance.** Acceptance means that you start where you are and meet others where they are. Begin with self-acceptance. When you can accept yourself and others as you are and realize that wholeness includes your imperfections, you are able to take the first steps toward forgiveness. You can move forward with confidence and ease as you contribute your unique gifts to the creation of True Community.

    In your close relationships, how open are you to meeting the other person where they are, without judgment and with forgiveness?

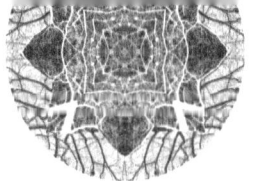

> In dwelling, live close to the ground.
> In thinking, keep to the simple.
> In conflict, be fair and generous.
> In governing, don't try to control.
> In work, do what you enjoy.
> In family life, be completely present.
>
> Lao Tzu

Going Deeper: Strengthening Bonds

DO YOU HAVE A STRONG COMMUNITY of support? A community of support is typically made up of a subset of the family and friends you interact with on a day to day basis. These are people with whom you have close relationships—people you can depend on to stand by you through good times and challenging times alike.

Your community of support includes those you would feel free to call on in times of need. These are people who offer emotional support, kindness, encouragement, compassion, and honesty. They include those with whom you feel free to be vulnerable and honest. These may be family members, close friends, church members, or neighbors.

Authentic relationships are reciprocal. They involve giving and receiving. A strong community of support can help you feel affirmed, supported, and resilient. As you are held in love and support by others, open your heart to offer loving support to others around you.

Focus Questions: *Family & Friends*

Reflect on the following focus questions to return to the experience of True Community through a deeper connection to family and friends. In your journal, write your responses to the following three questions:

- Who would I include in my community of support?

- If my community of support includes very few people, what actions can I take to expand that community?

- How am I showing up for others who may need my special support?

Clear Communication

One of the most important components of strong and resilient relationships is open and clear communication. Yet, many relationships are strained and broken by ineffective communication. Relationships involve two or more people, and it takes more than one person in any relationship dynamic to have clear communication.

To facilitate better communication, remember the importance of holding space in your closest one-on-one relationships. It is in that potent and fertile space between two or more people that real relationship and connection can take root and thrive. In that spaciousness, there is greater opportunity for exploring the underlying needs of each participant in the relationship. Through an abiding commitment to create spaciousness in your relationships, you are better able to find the common ground which will lead you and others to deeper compassion and understanding for one another.

Tension and emotions can run high in relationships in which one partner expects the other to be a mind reader or to automatically tune in to what the other is thinking and needing. To avoid such a circumstance in your closest relationships, consider these questions:

- Have I ever felt hurt or disappointed when my partner seemed aloof or unaware of my needs and wants?

- How might that relationship have been different if I had been more open and clear about what I was really needing in the moment?

- Where have I expected the other person to be a mind reader or know what I was thinking or needing?

Authenticity and Difficult Conversations

Being your authentic self extends to all areas of your life, including your communication with others. If we are to bring authentic communication to our closest relationships, we must be willing to enter into unknown territory. At some point you may need to step outside your comfort zone to have a difficult or challenging conversation with someone.

Your willingness to engage in such a conversation can be a gauge to how meaningful the relationship is to you. There is no guarantee about the outcome of difficult conversations. Difficult conversations require a foundation of love and vulnerability, of courage and commitment. When you engage in a high-stakes conversation, you risk losing something that holds special meaning for you. In fact, it is possible that you may lose the relationship itself.

Authentic relationships require that we care deeply enough to risk the relationship and that we act from a place of love for ourselves and for the other person. The difficult conversations referred to here are not about tough love; rather, such conversations are about committing to authentic communication from a place of unconditional love in service to the greater good of both parties.

Having a difficult conversation is a clear choice to take positive action rather than continue to ignore what needs to be said. A difficult conversation may be needed in order to clear the air or to reach greater clarity and understanding of an unresolved issue between two or more people. Having a difficult conversation may be awkward and even unpleasant, but the outcome is almost always worth it. The long-term benefits of such a conversation outweigh the short-term unpleasantness.

The key to authentic communication when such difficult conversations become necessary is to avoid blame and judgment. Approach the conversation from a place of loving concern for yourself, for the other person, and for the relationship. How willing are you to engage with a family member or close friend in a difficult conversation?

Considerations for Difficult Conversations

Let's take a closer look at some of the considerations that come into play with regard to authenticity and difficult conversations in close relationships. When you need to have an important conversation with a friend or family member, consider the following:

Conflict. Relationships by their nature are not simple. In fact, they can be layered with a complexity that, while challenging, actually adds dimension and depth to your life. Close relationships may trigger stressful reactions and conflict. Self-awareness can help you explore your own triggers that, if left unchecked, may lead to emotional outbursts and conflict.

Self-awareness can also open you up to a deeper understanding of others' needs and emotional triggers. By being more aware of your own triggers, you can more easily anticipate which situations may lead to an unwanted reaction. With greater awareness and practice you can learn to allow for space between the sudden trigger and your default response. The space you create becomes a space of awareness and healing.

When you have reacted in the moment, with a violent or other unwanted outburst, the damage is done. At this point, it is too late to undo it or take it back. Allow yourself to drop into a space of awareness, so that the raw edges of your emotions can be softened. Holding this space even for a few moments allows you the space to pause and take a few breaths. Then, you are better equipped to see the situation for what it really is.

Letting Go. In one sense, letting go means you let go of your ego desire to control the other person or to set your own expectations for outcomes in their lives. Letting go has to do with your choice to take responsibility for your own choices and actions while also allowing others the freedom to make their own choices. In this sense, letting go is about releasing.

Letting go may also hold a meaning that is similar to surrender. Seen from this perspective, you allow yourself to let go and fall into the spaciousness of the relationship. You feel held and safe in the relationship, so you can lean into it without judgment and experience it as it unfolds.

Clear Values. Our values reflect what we hold as important and meaningful. Gaining clarity about your values helps you know more about yourself. This leads to the ability to make informed choices, including decisions about who you choose to form close bonds with.

In terms of family, knowing your values adds richness to interactions and helps you to become a more positive role model for your children and others. Children learn from the examples we set, and the values that undergird your life and decisions are communicated to your children and others in the context of family. Enhanced clarity about your values can guide you in the decisions you make as a parent or family member.

The Golden Rule. *"Do unto others as you would have them do unto you."* The Golden Rule that many of us learned as children holds much practical truth. Its wisdom is applicable in all of our interactions, to include those with family and close friends. When we live by the Golden Rule, we treat others with the same respect we would want them to show us.

Feelings Awareness. What are you feeling right now in this moment? Can you name the feeling? You might be surprised about how many people are unaware of their true feelings. As humans we have a broad range of feelings, and these feelings are a natural part of who we are.

Some of us were raised to think that certain feelings and emotions were unacceptable. Because of this, we learned to repress or stuff those feelings. Two examples of subtle messages we may send our children that can cause them to mistakenly think what they are feeling is not ok are:

Boys don't cry
It's wrong to feel angry.

Stuffing or denying feelings affects us emotionally and physically. Knowing our feelings and having the freedom to express them appropriately is important for overall well-being and contributes to our everyday interactions with others. When we honor all of who we are, that naturally includes our feelings. All feelings are okay. How we act out our feelings may not be okay, especially if our actions bring harm to ourselves or others.

When interacting with your children, it is important to affirm and honor what they are feeling. This parenting practice teaches children that feelings are valid and helps them be able to distinguish between the range of feelings that may arise. If your child is angry, you may ask the child a question like, "Are you feeling angry because...?" Or you might turn that into a statement such as, "I'm noticing you are angry." Helping your children name their feelings helps validate their experience.

Recognizing Needs. Our feelings are closely related to our needs. When your needs are being met, you generally experience positive emotions and feelings. When your needs are not being met, negative feelings tend to arise. A part of understanding and honoring our feelings is recognizing what we are needing in any given situation.

- Can I think of a recent situation in my family life in which tempers flared and conflict erupted?
- What feelings were being expressed?
- What might have been the unmet needs underlying the conflict that arose?

In heated moments of conflict, it is often difficult to pause long enough to create a safe space between the trigger to conflict and our reaction or response. Yet, the truth is, you always have a choice about how open and expansive the space you create is. At the ground of that space is the energy of love. This is the meaning of holding space for ourselves and others. When we hold space, there is room for love to be expressed.

Needs vs. Neediness. Everyone needs to be seen, heard, and feel as if they really matter. When our needs are met in our relationships, conflict is minimized and the relationship can grow. That said, it is important to see the distinction between needs and neediness. Everyone has needs. Needs are universal. When we can recognize what it is we are needing in a certain situation, we can better make choices about how to best get these needs met in positive ways.

Neediness, on the other hand, is associated with perceived lack and is rooted in deep-seated fear. Neediness stifles us. Decisions made and actions taken from a sense of lack or neediness are often grasping and desperate. For example, jealousy stems from neediness. It is a reaction to a core fear of abandonment and the feeling of not feeling loved. It can destroy relationships as the jealous person desperately attempts to hold on to the person they fear may abandon them.

Life Learning through Relationships

Life is a journey of learning and growing, and every circumstance in our lives offers a new opportunity to expand our awareness and increase our impact in the world. But did you also realize that in your relationships with others you are also a teacher?

This realization that we learn through relationships can add an exciting new dimension to your interactions with others. As you bring this awareness of being both learner and teacher into all your relationships, you may see that you are perceiving others with less judgment and more forgiveness. As seen through the eyes of the True Self, relationships become more about giving and receiving and we enter more easily into the natural flow of life.

You always have choices. In every circumstance you have the power to make a choice. This may be surprising to you, because there may have been situations in your life where you felt boxed in and as if you had no choice. Thinking that you have no choice can cause you to feel hopeless.

Each one of us has the power of choice whether we realize it or not. Even opting not to choose is a choice! Simply realizing that we do have the power to choose is empowering. As much as you may want to be in control and influence others to do what you think is best for them—and for you, it is important to understand that you can only be responsible for your own decisions and actions.

Family Connections: Context and Continuity

Perhaps your strongest and most powerful connections are those you have with family members. In the best experiences of family, family brings a sense of belonging. Your family connections also provide you with context for your life and a sense of continuity over time. A sense of family can ground us in our place in the world. These aspects of our relationship to our family affirm to us that we hold an important space in the world—that we matter.

Family life based on the flow of love provides an open and spacious environment of nurturing where family members are seen and heard. In such an environment, family members feel that they really matter and are affirmed for their innate preciousness and goodness. A close bond with your family can provide the necessary foundation for the cultivation of community. Presence to our relationships with individual members of our family will enhance our experience of True Community within the family.

Connecting with Your Childhood Experience

How would you describe your childhood? When you think back to your childhood, what feelings come up for you? What is your childhood story? Is it a happy one or is it a story of shame? Of triumph or tragedy?

For some, childhood is a time of innocence, happiness, playfulness, and wonder. For others, their childhood experience is filled with less happy memories and sometimes even trauma and tragedy. Over time, family stories and memories of childhood can become mythologized in our collective telling and retelling.

We cannot change what happened in our past, but we can reframe aspects of the story in our minds. For example, if you see yourself as a victim in your story, how might you reframe that story? Perhaps you could choose to focus on the lessons learned. Or perhaps you could focus on how the pain and suffering of your childhood made you more resilient and determined.

What if you chose to tell the story of how challenging circumstances led you to create a better experience for your own children? Retelling your story in this way is empowering. Rather than taking your power away and consistently casting yourself in the role of victim, you become the hero of your life. How we see ourselves has an impact on all our relationships, to include our closest one-on-one relationships with family members and close friends.

For families with recurring cycles of neglect or abuse, it is important to find ways to change the pattern. One of the best ways to do what you can to break negative cycles is to see it for what it is and choose a new path forward. Consider the following questions:

- What is my responsibility to change my family story?
- What can I do to interrupt that vicious cycle?
- How can my choices today ensure that my retelling of my story is not defined by continual pain and suffering?
- How will I write a new story, beginning today?

Healing childhood wounds requires that we come to terms with what happened and integrate that into the wholeness of who we are at our true center. Take time to carefully consider what you can do to accept what happened and integrate what was learned from the experience. Consider the following questions:

- What can I do to begin the healing of the wounds of my childhood?
- How might reframing my family story strengthen my bonds of connection with family members and friends today?
- How might reframing my place in the story from one of victimhood to one where I become the hero in an epic life learning experience make forgiveness possible for me and my family members?

True Connection with Children

Your childhood experiences greatly affect your capacity for parenting your own children. That is one reason that your dedication to a path of healing holds such importance. Your childhood experiences affect how you view the world and how you interact in it. Quite possibly they contribute to your current mindset about being a parent.

If you are a parent or even if you are not a parent but have children in your extended family, consider these questions:

- What is my mindset about parenting? How do I feel about children and about being a parent?
- Do I view my role as a parent to control my children and mold them according to my own expectations? Or do I have a more expansive view of parenting?
- Do I think children should be seen and not heard? Do I intentionally create a space for self-discovery and self-value for my children and, where possible, for other children in my extended family?

Wholly Connected Parenting

Connection with your True Self can open your eyes to the wonder and awe of parenting. It can allow you to become a witness to your child's growing up years, rather than controlling how that unfolds. Your children are not property to be controlled and manipulated or shown off when convenient or beneficial to you. When your connection to your True Self is strong and you have examined your own childhood experiences, you see your children and the children around you as precious gifts placed in your care.

Children need clear boundaries. They need to feel supported and protected. Yet, they also need the freedom to discover and express their truth in the world. Your role as a parent is to support and guide them in an environment where they can learn and grow.

Children are not miniature replicas of their parents. They are each precious and unique. Your interaction and BE-ing with your children as they grow can lead to some of the most rewarding times in your life—if you make the conscious choice to be present to them and their process.

Here are some quick tips that will support true connection with your children and all children:

- Kindle the flame of your child's curiosity
- Help them to connect with an authentic expression of self
- Encourage their playfulness, innocence, and joy
- Nurture them so that they know love and develop trust
- Encourage them to explore their world
- Cultivate curiosity, wonder, and awe
- Treat them with kindness and tenderness
- Tell them how precious they are
- See them as sacred
- Affirm their intrinsic value
- Hold a space of openness where they can learn and grow
- Look in their eyes
- Smile at them every chance you have
- Adore them as you watch them sleep
- Affirm their feelings as real and true
- Be a good role model
- Live in integrity and honesty
- Allow them to be the children that they are
- Avoid unreasonable expectations

- Avoid placing unnecessary responsibilities on them
- Provide their basic physical and emotional needs
- Be nonjudgmental with them
- Avoid judgment of others
- Be fully present with your child
- Listen intently and deeply
- Follow your inner wisdom and guidance
- Meet challenges with vulnerability and courage
- Be pleasant
- Communicate openly and honestly
- Recognize and honor their needs
- Do the very best you can

Children can teach us so much about simply BE-ing in the world. Open yourself to experience childlike playfulness and joy. That joy exists at all times within you. You simply need to allow it to express itself. Notice children at play, and observe their sense of joyful abandonment. Listen to their laughter. Dare to let go and play *with* your children. Open yourself to share their wonder as you introduce them to new experiences and teach them to engage with the world around them.

Parenting with Grace

It is easy to judge yourself as a parent and to judge or berate yourself for perceived parenting mistakes. Be gentle with yourself as you parent your children and engage with children in society. Practice self-compassion. Acknowledge that you are not perfect. Congratulate yourself for doing the very best that you can. Life is a journey—a process of growing and learning. Being a parent is one rewarding dimension of your complex life.

If you are filled with judgment and blame toward your parents for the way they parented you, you may find yourself consumed by negative thoughts and self-talk that casts you as a victim. Most parents simply do the best they know how to do as parents.

- Understanding this, can you accept that your parents were not perfect, forgive them, and move on with your life?

- Can you begin to see your parents through eyes of loving compassion?
- How might you channel your own experience into a fierce determination to parent your own children with greater awareness and understanding?

The life lessons you learn as a parent can be applied to all areas of your life, including your relationships with your friends and close connections. The potential for True Community is strengthened as you show up fully as a loving and responsible parent. Parenting with grace is a challenge at times, but the reward is well worth the effort.

Intimate Relationships

For intimate relationships to be resilient and endure, they need to be built on love, trust, and tenderness. Kindness, acceptance, and friendship are other characteristics of thriving intimate relationships. Intimate relationships can be complex, but when they are built on a foundation of love they are more likely to be able to withstand the challenges that arise from misunderstandings and conflict.

All relationships need space for intimate partners to grow and thrive, and freedom and spaciousness are present in strong and loving relationships. In spite of a common misconception, living from your True Self means that you embrace the growth and development of those around you. When we are connected to our authenticity, we naturally bring greater freedom into our relationships with others.

Sometimes really loving another person means that we must allow them the freedom to explore. In love, we may choose to let them go so that they can continue their life's journey without us. As painful as that situation may be, as a self-aware person we know we cannot control other people's lives. Nor do we want to.

Likewise, you cannot make another person love you. This can be a difficult lesson to learn. As we connect more fully with our inner truth and expand our connection with others, we realize that jealousy and clinging to others is not true love. Rather, these are acts of desperation driven by the fear or terror of losing the other person.

Jealousy and other unhealthy behaviors in relationships are symptomatic of an underlying emotional neediness. In contrast, emotional well-being is rooted in truth and love.

Honoring Our Elders

What is your mindset about growing older? What feelings or emotions come up for you when you think about getting older? What is your relationship with your elders? What is your relationship with your grandparents and other older adults in your life? The way we treat older people speaks volumes about our own level of self-awareness and development. When we open our hearts to true connection, we expand our capacity to embrace all of humanity and will naturally want to extend our loving support to everyone. As your relationship with your True Self is enriched, your capacity to extend yourself to include and embrace others, including the elderly, is expanded.

When you feel connected within, you can experience joy in all relationships. With a new vision of deeper awareness, you embrace everyone as belonging to one humanity. You recognize and honor the contributions of each individual, including older people who often are ignored or dismissed as they age. When you are connected you look upon your elders as holders of great wisdom from the long and rich experiences of their lives. You welcome closer connection with seniors from your circle of family and friends.

Showing deep respect for our elders affirms their intrinsic worth as part of the whole of humanity and the world. Entering into relationship with aging adults also provides opportunities for learning for younger generations. As you model love, acceptance, and inclusion, you teach your children and others about the ongoing cycle of life and death. This helps us all to realize that growing older and dying is a natural and beautiful part of our being in the world.

True Connection with Older Adults

Having a senior family member or friend living in your home can add a new layer of connection. Similarly, having an older parent or grandparent share your home can help them feel loved and affirmed.

While you help provide for their physical needs, allowing them to be a part of your family life keeps them connected with those they love and cherish.

Realistically, we know that conflicts may arise in any relationships. Conflicts involving seniors can be especially difficult and stressful. These conflicts may be due to underlying and unresolved issues, or they may be due to the everyday stresses that life can bring. All relationships are complex and layered. Coming to older adults with an open heart paves the way for strengthening your relationship with them. Recognizing your own needs in these relationships is important, and self-care practices can give you the space to refresh and renew.

Older generations are holders of deep wisdom from which we can all benefit and be enriched. When we shut aging adults out of our lives or ignore them altogether, we are cutting ourselves off from a wellspring of wisdom from which we can learn. Here are some ideas for embracing elders in your community in ways that enrich their lives as well as your own:

- Treat them with kindness and respect
- Offer your support and help, if needed
- Tell them how much they mean to you
- Express interest and curiosity about their life
- Invite them to share their stories with you
- Create a loving, supportive space for connection
- Notice signs of loneliness or depression
- Honor their need to be seen and heard
- Show them that they matter to you and to others

What is your relationship with your ancestors? This question may seem odd to you, but our relationship to the generations that have come before us does matter. Having some knowledge about your ancestors can add context and a sense of continuity for your life. Knowledge about your ancestors can enhance your sense of who you are. Knowing the story of your ancestral lineage and family heritage can help you feel connected with those who lived long before you.

What is your level of curiosity about your ancestors? What fears do you hold about learning more about your family heritage? What excites you about this idea? Consider small steps you can take to learn more about your family lineage and those who came before you.

Healing Broken Relationships

Not all relationships are expressions of love, trust, and openness. Some relationships can be quite toxic. Is it your responsibility to try to heal toxic or broken relationships? First, know that you cannot expect to change other people. You can only change your reactions and the way in which you respond to others. You can choose how you act, but you cannot make others act in the way you might like them to act. Others take actions based on their own choices.

For some relationships, the best choice is to accept that you have done what you can to connect in a positive way. You cannot control the choices of the other person or make others act in the same way. You can accept the situation, view it with compassion and forgiveness, and then move on. Remember that every relationship is a learning opportunity.

Questions to consider when you are facing a broken or unhealed relationship:

- What is the learning I have received from this relationship?
- How have I grown from this relationship?
- How can I open myself to forgiveness in this situation?

True Friends

Even though you may have a large group of persons you consider friends, you may only have one or two people who you consider true friends. With these individuals, you share especially close and trusting relationships, and these friendships add richness and meaning to your life. In the close circle of a few friends—or sometimes just one special friend—you feel assured that there is someone who is always there for you. Your capacity to embrace true friends in the spaciousness of love and non-judgment opens you to a fuller experience of the world.

Are you a true friend to anyone? How would you describe a true friend? In what ways is a relationship with a true friend different from or similar to any other friendship? Take a few moments to review these characteristics that might describe a true friend, then add your own characteristics to this list.

A true friend is...
- Loyal—will stand up for you
- Dependable—there for you in good times and bad
- Encouraging
- Honest
- Trustworthy
- Non-judgmental
- Compassionate

Practices for Connection: Family & Friends

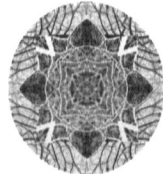

THIS CHAPTER OFFERS PRACTICES to ground you in your experience of your family and close relationships. Refer to these practices and the questions for deeper reflection as you continue to strengthen your connection to your family members and close friends in the coming months and years.

Beginning with Gratitude

Strong and resilient relationships with others don't just happen. They require conscious nurturing and ongoing maintenance to ensure they will last. In addition to the valuable lessons from our lived experience, meaningful connections with others are enhanced the more we engage with others in ways that are conscious and intentional. The following gratitude practices are simple, practical exercises to help you do just that.

- ✓ **Gratitude for Family Connections.** Tonight before you go to bed, write down three ways that you feel especially connected to your family. Silently express gratitude for your family connections.

- ✓ **Gratitude for Children.** Consciously practice being fully present with your child or a child in your extended family. The next time your child asks you a question or seeks your attention, sit down with them. Meet the child on his or her level. Give your full attention to him or her and listen deeply. Look into the child's eyes. Be fully present. Every night after your child has fallen asleep, go to her bedside and watch her sleep. Adore her beautiful face of innocence. Feel gratitude in your heart for your precious child and your special connection with her. Set an intention to be fully present with your child each and every day.

- ✓ **Gratitude for Community.** Create a *Community of Support Map*. On a large piece of paper, create a graphic that maps out your community of support. Start by drawing a circle in the middle of the paper. Label that circle "ME," realizing that you are the center of your community of support. Then, sit quietly as you consider who among your family and close friends make up your support network. Who do you feel close to? Who can you call on in times of need? Who do you have fun with? Who do you really trust? Write the names of those who make up your support network by how close you consider they are to you. After you complete the map, take few minutes to reflect on it. How do you feel as you view your social support network? How supported do you feel? Who did you put closest to you on the map? Take a few moments to feel gratitude for those you feel most supported by.

- ✓ **Gratitude for Elders.** Our need to be heard and seen and to know we matter does not diminish as we get older. Honoring the elders in our community helps meet their need for affirmation, meaning, and recognition. Set the intention today to connect with an elderly person in your circle of family or friends. Sit with that person. Ask them if they would share a happy memory from their childhood, perhaps beginning with one important lesson they have learned in life. Or invite them to share something on any topic they would like to share. One idea is to invite an elder to participate with you in Story Corps. For more information on Story Corps and to find a recording story booth location near you, please visit www.StoryCorps.org.

- ✓ **Gratitude for Ancestors.** Write a letter of gratitude to one of your ancestors. You may not know their names or anything at all about them or the lives they lived, but without your ancestors having lived their lives, you would not be here. Expressing your gratitude for them can remind you of a lineage of connection that adds context and meaning to your life.

✓ **Gratitude for Close Friends.** Set an intention to tell a close friend how much his or her friendship means to you. Consider doing this for all of your close relationships. Make a date with yourself to express your appreciation in unique ways. The next time you are with a close friend, take the time to express your gratitude for their friendship. Going the extra mile to communicate your gratitude for a friend's presence in your life will enhance and strengthen those relationships.

Nurturing and Maintaining Relationships

Just like a flower garden requires ongoing attention, our relationships require our tender loving care in order to take root, grow and thrive. Following are two creative activities for reflection on your relationships with family and friends. The first is a fun and creative art project about tending the garden of your relationships. The second is a journaling practice that invites you to reflect on your relationships for greater understanding, growth, and change.

✓ **My Family and Friends Art Garden.** For this project, you will need the following materials:
- 8.5" x 11" sheet of paper
- large piece of paper (from sketch book or other sturdy paper larger than 8.5" x 11" if available)
- color pens, pencils or markers

This art project does not require any special artistic skills or previous art experience. Spend a few minutes thinking about your family members and friends. List their names on your sheet of paper. These people make up your current family and friend relationship garden. Think about each person on your list. Ask the following questions as you consider each person:

- *What makes them special to you?*
- *Are there individuals on your list with whom you have a strained relationship?*
- *What color comes to your mind as you think about each person and your relationship?*
- *What kind of flower or plant best represents each one?*

Be creative with your garden. You may find it helpful to write down this information beside their name on your piece of paper. Remember to include yourself on your list as all your relationships include *you*. Next, on the large sheet of paper, use color pens, pencils or markers to draw a flower or plant to represent yourself in your garden. What color best represents you? Then draw and color a flower to represent each person on your family and friends list. Write each person's name on their respective flower or plant. As you work on your art project, consider these questions:

- *What is the reason that I chose this specific color to represent myself?*
- *What is the reason that I chose this specific color to represent each of my family and friends?*
- *Where is each person (flower) located in relationship to myself in my garden?*
- *Which persons (flowers) did I place closest to myself in my garden? What are the reasons I placed them closest to me? Who are the people who are farthest from me in my garden?*

- *Which of your relationships are firmly rooted?*
- *Are there any withering relationships in your garden that need your extra attention to help them grow and thrive? How might you tend to this relationship to see it thrive?*

Now take a big picture view of your relationship garden. How would you describe it? What feelings come up for you as you look at it? If your garden is small with few relationships, that is okay. Remember this is an artistic representation of your current garden. You can always add to your garden to make it larger. Or you may choose to focus your attention on strengthening and nourishing those beautiful relationships that are already yours. Finally, congratulate yourself for your creative artistic expression!

Note: As an ongoing practice, you may consider planting a real flower garden to represent your relationships with family and friends. In spring, summer, or fall, when your flowers bloom, give your flowers to your family and friends who are "planted" in your garden.

✓ **My Family and Friends Journal.** For this practice you will need a journal or a notebook and a writing instrument. You may choose to record in your journal electronically; however, the practice of handwritten journaling can help bring you to presence and involve you somatically in this self-expressive process. Set an intention to write in your journal on a regular basis. When you are intentional about your journaling, it can become a regular practice for you.

Use your journal to write about your relationships with your family and friends. This may seem awkward at first if you are new to journaling. The act of expressing yourself through journaling can be healing in itself.

Through journaling you may have new insights about your relationships. Reflecting on what you express in your journal may help you view your relationships in ways you had not previously considered. You can also use your relationship journal to express gratitude for your relationships. Be sure to date each journal entry so you can look back and see changes in your relationships over time.

21 Questions for Deeper Reflection

1. How would I describe my relationship with my family?
2. Are there aspects of my family life I want to change?
3. What about my family connections brings me joy?
4. What is one thing I can do today to nurture a better relationship with my child or another family member?
5. In thinking about a strained or conflicted relationship, what are my unmet needs in this relationship?
6. How do I hold space for my friends to grow? What is stressful for me about being a close friend?
7. How might changing my mindset about aging in general change the ways I interact with my aging parents?
8. How can I enrich the lives of seniors in my life around me or form a stronger relationship with an elderly person in my family?
9. What mindset(s) do I have about parenting? How open am I to considering alternative viewpoints?
10. What is one important life lesson I learned from my mother? From my father?
11. What is my relationship with my ancestors? What do I know about them? What do I feel about them?
12. What is my greatest fear about close relationships?
13. When I think of "family," who do I include? How does my family give me context and a sense of continuity in life? What feelings come up for me when I think about attending a large family reunion?
14. What is my relationship with my siblings?
15. What painful memories am I holding onto that may be holding me back? How can I make peace with them?

16. Who among my close relationships has been my greatest source of inspiration? Why?
17. Who is the person with whom I can be most authentic?
18. Who do I especially feel disconnected from? What is one step I can take to reconnect with this person?
19. What qualities or strengths do I have that help connect me with others?
20. How do I cultivate community by connecting to new friends? What is one thing I can do this week to cultivate a new friendship or relationship?
21. How am I showing up in my relationships with family and friends?

3
The Larger Community
Pathways to Connection

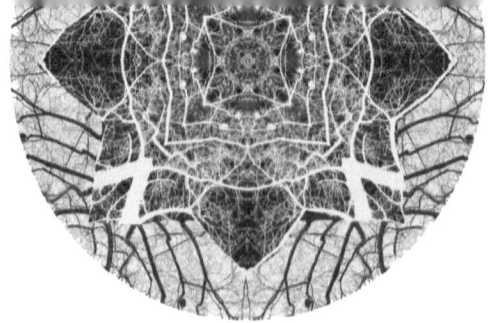

> The greatness of a community
> is most accurately measured by the
> compassionate actions of its members.
> Coretta Scott King

Local Connections

ALONG THE SPIRAL PATH with its five pathways for a return to True Community, the third pathway leads to a connection to the larger community. To connect to greater purpose and experience authentic community, it is important to connect intentionally to the local communities where you live, work, and play.

Consider the places you go, what activities you engage in, and who you see on a day to day basis:

- What are the natural communities you interface with as you engage in your everyday life and work?
- Where do you go where other people gather?
- Who or what kinds of people do you often encounter as you engage in your daily or weekly routines?

Natural Networks of Belonging

There are many natural networks of belonging that provide fertile ground for our experience of community. Begin by considering the place you call home. How can you connect to existing opportunities right in your neighborhood? What if you started something? Social and community clubs, centers of worship, and civic organizations offer opportunities to expand your social circle. Many community centers offer programs and events that provide ample opportunities to engage in the world around you and to experience greater meaning and purpose in your life.

Also consider your work life and career. How connected do you feel to your workplace and co-workers? Consider relationships and opportunities to build community in your workplace. From casual conversation around the water cooler to workplace social functions, there are likely already opportunities to connect to and cultivate community at work.

Each of these settings or situations offers an opportunity to connect to community and greater meaning in your life. Some examples might include places such as your local neighborhood, workplace, or worship center. Also consider schools, public parks, shops, and library. Think about the coffee shop you stop by, the grocery store, or the corner bakery. All of the places you frequent and the people with whom you come into contact hold potential for meaningful connection to your larger community. Let's look more closely at how we can cultivate these connections, beginning with what you naturally bring to your interactions with the people you encounter on a regular basis.

Community, One Person at a Time

Connecting through the pathway of your larger community allows you to extend the reach of your engagement and contribution in gentle and natural ways. It opens you to new possibilities for belonging in service to the greater good of your community beyond your family and close friends. These connections are made naturally when you become brave enough to share yourself—even in small ways.

Your connection with your local community and the people who share this space with you begins with and flows from your connection with your True Self. Through the simple choice to be open-hearted, the love you express naturally connects you to those around you. Your experience of inner wholeness extends outward to inspire others and to touch them in your daily interactions in your community.

Because any community is made up of dynamic relationships and is influenced by both our relationship with ourselves and our relationship with others, it is important to examine how we are valuing and honoring each relationship in our daily lives. As we each make the journey of self-discovery and awareness, we naturally come into greater alignment and an improved relationship with ourselves. This may be a new concept to some, but our relationship to self deeply impacts those around us. This includes family members, those in our local community, and ultimately the greater world. Of course, your relationship with yourself first impacts the way you view and treat yourself. And how you view and treat yourself significantly influences how you engage and interact with those you encounter on a regular basis.

Our relationship with ourselves also impacts the ways that we interact with nature, to include the nature of community. It all begins with you! As we come into deeper self-awareness, our love for self grows. This inner love naturally flows outward and is expressed in our relationships with family members, in our local community, and beyond.

Thriving communities value and respect all who live within them. As we respect and appreciate the unique contributions that every person makes to our community, we create a solid foundation for our community's future. True Community happens one person at a time and one decision at a time. As you move through your daily and weekly routine, practice conscious awareness of simple connections in your local community.

Reciprocity and Interconnectedness

The webs of connections within the larger community can be quite intricate. This complexity adds strength and resilience to the social fabric of the whole community. Many of the connections we make within community are connections with people we interact with on a day to day basis. Other relationships are situational or transactional in nature, having more to do with less-frequent engagements in the community. Yet, all of these relationships are important and add to the richness of our experience of community.

Our experience of community is much more satisfying and meaningful when we consciously cultivate relationships with an open-hearted intention to co-create meaningful connections. Regardless of their nature—whether social, financial or another type—our relationships in the larger community are reciprocal. They involve both giving and receiving. As you consider your own life and the web of interconnected relationships and the quality of reciprocity in those relationships, consider the following questions.

- What is my idea of community?
- When I reflect on the larger community where I live, what types of relationships naturally come to mind?
- How connected and engaged in my local community am I willing to be?
- How will I choose to be more involved?

Community and Belonging

Belonging to a group helps us to feel loved and valued for who we really are. Feeling affirmed and valued by community, we develop a sense of deep honoring for ourselves and for our community. When we have positive experiences over time, involvement in the larger community becomes a natural and welcoming experience. Communities arise from these bonds of trust among people who feel safe in their interactions with others. In community, people begin to feel connected. They begin to believe that they can rely on each other. As trust grows, the sense of community and *belonging* grows.

When we know that we have meaningful contributions to make, the community becomes a better place for everyone. Making a unique contribution to community requires conscious effort and personal responsibility. Being a responsible contributor in your community starts with an honoring and support of what that community stands for. Responsibility only happens when community members are able to be honest and authentic in their interactions with one another and when they act with integrity and in alignment to the shared values of the community.

As your desire to connect awakens and expands, your understanding of *belonging* in the larger community becomes more apparent. So does your commitment to being an engaged and responsible member of the larger community. A thriving community is composed of people who are consciously engaged in making a better community possible for everyone. Being responsible means that you own your decisions and actions without blaming others or making excuses for your choices or failure to choose. When you are responsible, you accept the consequences of your own actions and willingly demonstrate your valuing of the community through your valuable contribution to the larger group.

Cultivating Compassion and Resilience

Compassion is a hallmark of a thriving community. Out of love and compassion comes the natural desire to serve others. As you begin to see yourself in the eyes of all others, you recognize the sacredness of all life. As self-awareness deepens, you sense the innate connection and unity of all life. You see that we are connected as one imperfect but sacred humanity. As you come more into this understanding of life, you begin to see that your desire to help or support one person benefits the whole.

The well-being of the community as a whole is dependent upon the involvement of those who feel connected to that community and consider it *home.* As you connect to your inner truth, you will naturally find new meaning in community. Your unique way of engaging in your community may inspire other individuals and families to find greater meaning and purpose through a reconnection to their local communities.

> Resilient communities are inclusive and value diversity. There is no place for "otherness" that serves only to divide and weaken the community.

Connecting to community takes many forms, but a deep desire to connect and express yourself within the local community grows stronger as you connect to your true center. As you expand your connection to the larger community, you will discover that the 12

Key Characteristics for Resilient Relationships also apply in interactions within the larger community. We can really *be* in community as we consciously cultivate these key characteristics within ourselves and begin to manifest them in our external lives. We do that as we interact and engage with others in local communities.

Characteristics of True Community Revisited

As you travel The Spiral Pathway of Connection and experience the wholeness of community, you may notice that each of the five pathways begins with you. For a return to True Community experienced along each pathway, we begin with the True Self. Regardless of which pathway you choose, if you consciously and intentionally travel along any of these five pathways, you are led deeper into the experience of wholeness and integration, which is a hallmark of True Community.

As a reminder, True Community is characterized by the following eight key characteristics:

- Connection and Community
- Wholeness and Integration
- Action, Expansion, Engagement
- Truth and Alignment
- Nature and Natural Systems
- Peace and Compassion
- Sustainability
- Inclusivity

The full experience of the True Self along The Spiral Path of Connection is like a holographic experience. As each of the five spirals *un*fold and *en*fold, each spiral contains its own seed truth of the overall journey. The ultimate destination for each pathway is the same—True Community and the realization of being wholly connected. But each pathway provides a unique experience of wholeness and connection. Wholeness is inherent within each of the five pathways, and each pathway allows us to experience the wholeness that is already ours.

When we experience True Community, we are experiencing the wholeness of who we are in the context of the world and beyond. So long as you begin your journey with the inner journey to the True Self, your journey on the pathway of the larger community and each of the other connection pathways leads to the direct experience of True Community. In community, we become aware and connected and have the opportunity to fully align our lives with the continued and ever-expanding experience of wholeness and thriving.

The Joy of Community

When we are connected with our inner truth, we return to an experience of our natural state of joy. Joy is always present within each of us; we have merely forgotten it in the busyness of life up to now. In community, we are reminded of our natural state of joy, peace, and harmony. We remember the unity within ourselves and with the world.

Living in community becomes a grounding experience of the truth of who we really are. In community with others our joyful and playful state is amplified and expanded. Thriving communities realize the importance of togetherness. As such, they offer varied opportunities for connection. Examples of such opportunities might include leisure and recreation programs, local activities, public spaces and community parks for gathering with family and friends or convening community events or holiday celebrations open to any and all who wish to participate.

Thriving communities consciously plan events and other opportunities that naturally bring the whole community together for events such as holiday celebrations, parades, and commemorations. These gatherings are opportunities for the individuals, families, and groups that comprise the larger community to gather around a shared purpose. Such gatherings help build a sense of community pride and belonging and increase the experience of joy.

Look for unique opportunities to connect with others in joyful togetherness. For example, you might make it a higher priority to connect with your neighbors and make new friends by attending neighborhood social gatherings, such as block parties or group activities sponsored by a homeowners' association. If your neighborhood does not already host such events, what steps are you willing to take to help coordinate a fun and inclusive event?

Barriers to Connecting to the Larger Community

While some people fully embrace opportunities for connecting to the larger community, many more are hesitant to get involved. Most often, these individuals simply don't know where to begin. Faced with either an overwhelming number of options or not knowing what's available in our own communities, many of us fall into patterns of complacency and don't even venture out of our homes. Others may have ideas about how they could connect, but in the busyness of life feel they do not have time to make additional connections outside of family and close friends.

What is keeping you from a more fulfilling experience of connection to the larger community? What can you do to remove this barrier? Set an intention to take one practical step to overcome the barriers to fulfilling and joyful connections in your local community. Set aside time on your calendar to peruse what's happening in your local community. Decide to get involved in a way that feeds your soul.

Thriving communities are defined by the level of commitment individuals and families have to breaking through perceived barriers to bringing their whole hearts to the heart of community. There are both inner and outer journeys at play. The outward expression of your heart is what creates momentum and growth in the larger community. The more of us who commit to expressing who we are and sharing that with others within the larger community, the stronger the bonds between individuals, families, and groups within the community as a whole.

Simple Ways to Make a Difference Now

Here are some simple and adaptable ways to be an involved member of the community and begin to make a real difference every day.

- ✓ **Be Curious. Express Gratitude.** Thriving communities are formed when members of the community are open-hearted, curious, and engaged. Take the time to have a conversation with a neighbor. Share a smile or a word of encouragement. Go to the park or another public place and strike up a conversation with someone you don't know. Write a letter of appreciation to a public servant. Seek out information on local issues and initiatives and find creative ways to contribute your own ideas and talents.

- ✓ **Smile!** A smile is a powerful connector. In fact, a simple smile is considered the most powerful all of human gestures. Even when you feel rushed in your daily life, you can always smile at others. You never know how the smile you give to someone may brighten their day and make a real difference in how the rest of their day goes. Smiling benefits you, too—sometimes as much as it does the recipient of your smile. Your smile coveys feelings of happiness, acceptance, and warmth. The act of smiling releases important mood-enhancing chemicals while at the same time reducing stress-inducing chemicals. Smiling even helps reduce high blood pressure. Mother Teresa said, "Peace begins with a smile." With this powerful information in mind and heart, the next time you are out in your neighborhood, try out the power of your smile!

- ✓ **Keep it Local.** Commit to buying locally grown food. Support local merchants and artisans. Buying locally provides opportunities to make close and lasting friendships with local farmers and business owners. Your community thrives when more of your dollars stay in the local community. Register to vote. Learn about city and county issues, needs, and opportunities. Attend local workshops and events. Show your appreciation for each person's unique contributions to the community as you bring forward your own true voice and gifts. Pass on great finds in the community to others in your circles, and speak with pride about your local community and the ways it contributes to your life.

- ✓ **Look Out for Others**. Remember, thriving communities are compassionate communities. Help out those who might need assistance—an elderly neighbor or a person with a disability, for example. Offer support with transportation or simply express your kindness. Find simple ways to offer your time and talents to individuals and groups. Being considerate and aware is the first step to creating a stronger community. Be a good neighbor.

  Offer to help out aging or neighbors with disabilities. As the number of senior citizens in our population grows, it is increasingly important that they be valued and respected as integral members of the community. Many seniors seek out opportunities to engage with others, while others may be disconnected and feel lonely. Seniors who are respected and honored for their contributions both past and present are more inspired to continue to be engaged.

  What are some ways you can connect with seniors in your community? Could you help pick up a loaf of bread or sweep the sidewalk? How might you cultivate connections with people who live near you? Be creative. See how you feel about your community when you express concern for the people who share it with you.

- ✓ **Be Mindful of Your Footprint.** Live consciously and do the right thing. The ways that we show up in our community life is a matter of our personal choice and preference; however, in connection with your True Self, your sense of personal responsibility to always do the right thing for the good of the larger community becomes stronger. This desire arises from our sense of oneness and compassion for all others.

One way we can do the right thing by our community is to choose to live in an intentional and sustainable way. Take pride in keeping your private space and shared community spaces clean and welcoming. Consider all the ways you are receiving from community resources. Then, find simple ways to give back. Recycle. Donate to a nonprofit organization. Volunteer your time. Live simply to simply live.

✓ **Be a Mentor.** Mentoring can happen in both formal and informal ways. From taking a big step such as becoming a foster parent or adopting a child right down to simple actions such as volunteering for a local community nonprofit, your presence to others in the community is what matters most. Consider how you might share your knowledge, gifts, and talents with the younger generation or with specific populations within the larger society, such as the aging or persons with disabilities.

✓ **Show Compassion for Animals.** Your family might choose to rescue an animal or get involved in a volunteer organization that assists with providing care to animals. Communities are defined by how they treat those without a voice in the community. This extends to our furry friends or animals in your natural habitat that have been displaced or forgotten. If you have a heart for animals, reach out to a local animal rescue. Consider volunteering or adopting a pet in need.

✓ **Share Your Voice.** Consider convening a group to discuss issues that matter to you. This could happen in your local neighborhood or at the city-wide or even county-wide or regional level. Being a participant in local issues begins with finding ways to stay in touch with what's happening locally and sharing your unique perspective.

- ✓ **Commit to Personal Growth**. As you continue to grow yourself, you are also equipping yourself to get clear on ways you can contribute more fully to the community. This sets a great example in your own family and for other community members.

- ✓ **Volunteer.** Make it a goal to volunteer regularly in your local community. This puts you out in the community, where you are likely to hear about more opportunities for connection, engagement, and involvement than you ever knew existed! When you start exploring the opportunities for volunteering, you most likely will see that they abound in your community. Here is a quick list to help you get started:
  - Nonprofit organizations
  - Your child's school or a local educational institution
  - Local arts community (community theatre, museum)
  - Public libraries
  - Local election voting precincts
  - Your church, place of worship, or spiritual community

- ✓ **Become an Engaged Citizen.** Educate yourself on what's happening in your local community. Let your voice be heard by casting your vote in local and state elections. If you see a need, consider stepping up with others who care to meet that need. Consider running for an office in your local government where your voice, your ideas, and your skills can make a big difference.

The element of personal responsibility is inherent in the full experience of community. The form that your sense of personal responsibility takes may vary depending on the circumstances. As an engaged citizen it is our responsibility to take the personal actions that enrich the experience of community for everyone. When our experience of community includes civic life, we each may choose to take on formal responsibilities that contribute to the strength and resilience of the community. Here are some ways to experience community as an engaged citizen:

- Exercise your right to vote
- Encourage others to vote
- Volunteer to work at your local polling place
- Speak out for causes you care deeply about
- Attend local government meetings
- Be an informed citizen

✓ **Support Local Arts and Cultural Activities.** Get involved in the arts community as a volunteer. If you are an artist, consider expressing yourself creatively while you contribute to the cultural enrichment of the community.

✓ **Start a Community Garden.** Gardening is a wonderful way to bring people together to make connections with each other and with nature. Sharing in the bounty of a community garden reinforces the idea of what makes a community thrive: human connections, sustainability, and inclusion. Your community garden can serve as a model for a connected community. If your community currently does not have a garden, would you be willing to take a leadership role to explore the possibilities of creating a community garden?

✓ **Cultivate New Friendships.** Meeting people and cultivating new friendships can be regenerative and refreshing, adding richness to your life. As you connect more strongly with the True Self that resides at the center of your being, it becomes easier to open up to others. With a wider circle of friends comes opportunity for new experiences of learning and growth. Expand your circle of family and friends by engaging in experiences within the community. Meet new people through workshops and events that interest you. Go to community gatherings. Take time to identify creative ways you might meet people and cultivate friendships as you begin to make new connections in your community.

✓ **Plan a Potluck Supper.** Food brings people together. From ancient times, people have come together around communal meals. Today, potluck suppers and other shared meals are a regular event in many churches and community gatherings. Coming together with new friends around delicious food can add warmth and a sense of belonging in your life.

✓ **Be a Connector.** Some community organizations plan events designed to intentionally bring together diverse groups for conversation around important topics in order to bridge gaps, find common ground for understanding and compassion, and honor the wisdom and rich diversity of the groups. For example, a community nonprofit might host a community conversation in which senior citizens and teens come together for the purpose of bridging the generations through meaningful conversation and sharing a meal together. This kind of connection-building strengthens bonds and enriches the entire community.

✓ **Engage Teens and Young Adults.** Often communities overlook the unique contributions that teens and young adults can offer to enrich community connections. Their youthful energy, creativity, and unique generational insights are important enriching elements of the whole community. When planning community events, consider inviting teens and young adults to participate in planning, organizing, implementation, and follow-up. Including them as valued contributors to the whole of the community is affirming for teens and young adults. It builds trust and offers them the opportunity to make a difference in the community while also adding meaning and purpose during what can be a vulnerable stage in their lives. This early and active participation in community offers teens and young adults an invaluable experience, setting the stage for many to emerge as community leaders in the future.

In what ways could you serve as a connector to consciously bring people together for community conversations? Spend a few minutes now reflecting on some of the practical and simple steps you can take to connect to opportunities right in your backyard for a deeper, more fulfilling experience of community.

More Ways to Get Involved

If you are someone who yearns to experience and contribute to community in a more intense and extended way, there are a number of more involved ways to be engaged in the local community. If you have a passion for a particular cause or a product or service offering, here are two not-so-simple but meaningful ideas:

- ✓ **Become a Conscious Business Owner.** Have you ever considered starting your own small business? Business ownership is a great opportunity to engage in your community in ways that benefit you and your community. Starting a business in your community is a way to enrich your community through your own brand of business expression. Business ownership is not for everyone, but for those who are ready and willing to explore the possibilities, owning your own business can bring much personal satisfaction. It can result in closer connections with customers and other business owners, while making an economic contribution to the community.

    While being a business owner requires a high degree of personal responsibility and significant financial resources, it can bring meaning and purpose to your life.

Owning your own business offers opportunities to express your self creatively, especially if you choose to start a business in which you can highlight your creative talents and gifts. Further, as an entrepreneur you can model conscious business practices in your community. Be mindful of the type of business you establish. Take care to ensure it aligns with the values and norms of your local community and makes a valuable contribution to your community.

✓ **Start a Nonprofit Organization.** Do you have a passion for a social cause? Is there an unmet social need in your community? If so, you may want to consider founding a nonprofit organization. A first step in starting a nonprofit organization is to do extensive research to explore the feasibility and need in your community.

Nonprofits offer rich opportunities for people to get involved as volunteers and as recipients of the services of the organization. If you have the passion, skills, and support needed, founding and managing a nonprofit organization can provide deep meaning and purpose for your life while making a difference in your community.

If founding a new nonprofit is not for you, explore the rich opportunities to get involved in existing organizations in your community.

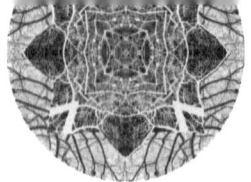

> There is no power for change greater than a community discovering what it cares about.
> Margaret J. Wheatley

Going Deeper: Intentional Connections

CONNECTION WITH OTHERS IS PART of our humanity, and the quality of our relationships with others makes for healthier and more robust communities. Within community we have so many options for getting involved in ways that honor our individual preferences and allow us to express who we really are. This chapter takes a deeper dive into the experience of True Community as we intentionally connect with our larger community in gratitude and with an expanded view of what is possible. As we open ourselves to a fuller experience of belonging in and to community, we can choose consciously how to strengthen our connection to the larger community.

Focus Questions: *The Larger Community*

Reflect on the following focus questions to return to the experience of True Community through your connection to your larger community. In your journal, write down your responses to the following three questions:

- How am I showing up in my larger community in ways that reflect who I really am?
- In what ways am I making a real difference in my larger community now?
- To what extent do I feel *at home* and that I really *belong* in my community?

Connect for Well-Being and Health

While you may have enjoyed the feeling of belonging that being engaged with community can bring, you may also have noticed that you simply feel better when you are connected with others. In fact, there is a growing body of research around the benefits of social connection as it pertains to health and well-being. As scientific evidence about the health benefits of connection mounts and is disseminated more broadly, our awareness of the importance of our relationships is heightened.

More and more we are coming to realize that our social connections do more than just make us feel good. We are social beings by nature, and our natural webs of connection wrap us in greater potential for overall well-being. As we avail ourselves of opportunities for connection with others, we embrace greater health, well-being, and thriving. With our increasing awareness of the importance of our connections, we can become more intentional about how we connect with others. With deeper awareness we can make more informed choices about our relationships so that we and others can enjoy the social, emotional and physical benefits that connection can bring.

Here are some of the ways that our social connections can benefit our health and well-being:

- **Happiness and Contentment**. Connection with others can result in increased happiness and contentment—positive emotions that have been shown to contribute to overall well-being. How do your current connections lead to the experience of happiness and contentment?

- **Reduced Depression**. Those who feel connected are less likely to experience loneliness and social isolation, which can lead to depression. It is commonly known that depression may also result in a neglect of physical needs such as personal hygiene, exercise, and nutrition—all of which can negatively impact health. When we begin to make more social connections, we become more trusting of ourselves and others. This sense of trust and safety increases the likelihood that we will expand our meaningful connections, which in turn results in a deepened sense of belonging and community.

- **Reduced Stress**. In the context of relationships, we often feel the support of others. Those who are connected with and can count on others for support feel less alone in dealing with the circumstances of their lives. Often, they experience less stress and anxiety.

- **Improved Physical Health and Increased Life Expectancy**. Loneliness and isolation can have negative effects on the cardiovascular and immune systems and are associated with a decreased life expectancy. With this awareness, we can be more mindful of connecting with others around us who may lack social connections. Senior citizens are a population segment particularly at risk. Elderly people who are connected to others who check in on them or bring them meals benefit from the companionship as well as the nutrition of the meals. Connection can bring hope, purpose, and meaning to their lives. How might you make a difference in the life of someone in your community who is socially isolated?

The Gift of Community

Community is a gift. True Community is realized as we open our hearts and are willing to connect with others. When we cultivate the inner and outer conditions in which community can thrive, connections emerge naturally.

Those persons engaged wholeheartedly in the local community continue to create opportunities for connection intentionally so the gift that is community may keep on giving. In community we can enjoy gifts such as sense of safety, of trust, of belonging, and of opportunity to grow and thrive. Each of us then has the power of choice to decide what other gifts we receive—and then give, depending on our willingness to receive and our personal preferences about how we wish to participate in the community.

Consider these questions about the gifts of community and your willingness to be involved:

- What are some of the gifts community has given me?
- How open am I to receiving the gifts of community?
- How am I contributing to the experience of community as a gift to others in my area?

Holding the space for community to emerge and receiving its gifts graciously is not always easy or simple. It involves conscious effort, awareness, openness, and a willingness to engage for the greater good of the whole community, to include yourself. True Community emerges from the shared values and aspirations of members of the community. Our personal responsibility is to help create the conditions that are conducive for the flourishing of community.

Sometimes community emerges from tragedy or suffering. When the heart is broken open, it creates the space for the emergence of community. In those circumstances community may be realized through experience of pain and through the inspiration of hope to recover from the tragedy. For example, after an event of human tragedy or disaster such as a hurricane, tornado, or mass shooting in which there is loss of life or property, those who experienced the tragedy often come together to help each other. This compassionate and empathetic coming together in response to a common tragedy, even in the face of own's own personal loss, helps to build community and togetherness. The community is strengthened and made more resilient as it comes together to heal.

Celebrating Community in Gratitude

Celebrating community includes pausing to acknowledge the gifts of community and express gratitude for what we have received. When we see ourselves as an integral contributor to community, we are more likely to notice the many benefits we might otherwise take for granted.

What are you grateful for when you consider your local community? Asking this question helps us become more aware of the intricate relationships woven into the rich fabric of the community. We are each a part of this rich fabric. When we celebrate the beauty and richness that each person contributes, to include our own contribution, we strengthen the bonds of community.

Community happens when we hold space for it to emerge naturally. When we impede the natural unfolding of what wants to emerge, we may see some form of community coalesce but it will inevitably fall short of its full potential. Communities that come together around economic or business relationships which are merely transactional lack the added richness of shared values and experiences among the community members. Unless community is allowed to emerge in the field of commonly held ideals, values, and conscious intentions, it will lack the strength and resilience of local networks and communities that are nurtured by compassion and love.

Community is about humanity in all its richness and diversity. Thriving communities are whole and vibrant with a richness that comes from the diverse lives of the members of the community and their connections with each other. We can look to examples from the natural world that demonstrate the resilience and diversity of community.

Nature thrives and flourishes most at the edges, in those places where different and diverse ecosystems come together. Communities, being integral in the natural world, are no different. Strength and resilience result from the coming together of diverse parts. A stronger, more creative system emerges from the effects of the complexity of the relationships interwoven in the space of the new system. The chaos and conflict of the original coming together becomes balanced in natural, self-regulating processes seen in the natural world.

Community as a State of Awareness

While we often think of community in physical terms, being in community is also a state of *awareness* of our connection with others. To be in community does not necessarily require that we are always in contact with others. Some people value solitude; yet, they may still be very connected to the community. These individuals may choose to engage by supporting community causes and buying locally, yet may spend most of their time in contented solitude apart from the community.

Solitude is a social choice, and they feel fulfilled and connected in the ways that matter to them. To be in community is not only about physical involvement. It is also a state of mind in which we hold the inner awareness that we are connected to others. We may go for extended periods of time without being in physical proximity to others. Yet, when we hold the awareness of our innate connection with others, we can lean into that knowing and find greater meaning and purpose through our awareness of our connectedness to one another and to the larger community.

Connection is a mindset based on awareness of your innate connection with all the world, to include your connections with other people. Those who have not yet become aware of their innate connection to others are less likely to experience connection to community. They may feel a sense of loss, isolation, and disconnection. Consider the ways a deeper awareness of your innate connection to all things and to your community can support you in times when a sense of loneliness creeps into your thoughts.

Your level of connection with your larger community is a matter of choice. Each community member has the power to choose how he or she wants to be engaged in the community. There are countless ways to engage, and the choices we each make are determined by such factors as personality, skills, talents, experience, wants, and needs.

The beauty of a thriving community is that it offers rich and varied opportunities for being involved in ways that benefit the individual contributor as well as the whole community. How do you choose to be engaged in your community?

Leadership Emerges Naturally in Community

Thriving communities in which everyone is welcome and valued need strong and compassionate leadership. As people come together in the connections that define community, leaders naturally emerge. Leaders demonstrate personal accountability and responsibility. They inspire the vision and direction that moves the community forward.

Depending on the type of community, leaders may be elected officials or individuals who stand out due to their skills, abilities, and desire to engage as leaders in non-elected leadership roles.

Are you a naturally emergent leader in your community? What are some of the main leadership characteristics you notice in existing community leaders? Are there unmet needs?

Community Response in Times of Need

Thriving communities are caring communities. People come together to support each other in good times and also in times of need. Circumstances such as natural disasters or personal losses including death, house fires, and hunger bring the community together to offer support to those in need. Grounded in compassion, the community responds out of a sense of love and the realization that we are all connected. What affects one person in the community affects all.

After personal losses and natural disasters, it is helpful for the community to hold space for healing. This can begin by listening deeply to those survivors, allowing them to tell their stories, when they are ready, in the warmth and loving space of acceptance and compassion. Coming together around those in need is a natural response to our compassionate hearts. How might you offer your support to a community neighbor who have survived a personal loss or other trauma?

Peaceful Hearts, Peaceful Communities

Peace begins within. Peaceful and compassionate communities emerge from the peaceful and loving hearts of those who call a community home. When conflicts arise, they are resolved peacefully by coming together to discover common ground where unmet needs can be acknowledged and understood and positive solutions can be reached.

Healthy, thriving communities set the expectation of non-violence in all interactions. A peaceful community also holds a vision of hope for a peaceful world. What is your personal responsibility for cultivating a more peaceful and compassionate community?

Cultivating New Ground

As our experience of community grows and evolves, we discover refreshing and creative ways to live and thrive together with greater purpose and meaning. While these experiments in community may seem new to many of us, they signify a return to a simpler, more connected way of life—a way of life where relationships and exchanges are based on trust, integrity, and generosity.

In our world today, we see that our modern technologies and systems, though in some ways making life more efficient and easy, have contributed to the breakdown of meaningful social connections, damaged the natural environment, and led to an imbalanced reliance on an economic system largely based on profit and greed. We are being invited to try creative ways of being and interacting together. These new ways of being in community are built upon the strength of relationships among people.

Rather than only a monetary value being placed on commercial exchanges, the webs of relationships are seen as adding value in terms of social capital. Below are some of the ways that communities are coming together creatively to explore new possibilities of living and exchanging goods and services. These new ways of being in community can contribute to a deeper experience of life.

> ✓ **Intentional Communities.** Intentional communities are residential communities that are consciously planned and created around some specific intention or purpose that benefits the whole community. Typically, these intentional communities are designed and organized so that community members live and work together for the benefit of the whole community. A community may have come together as a sustainable organic farming community or ecovillage, for example.

- ✓ **Shared Living Spaces.** As living costs rise, many people find that they are unable to afford the more traditional expectation of home ownership. Rental costs mean permanent housing is out of reach for many people, from young adults to senior citizens. More and more people are living together in shared spaces, sharing the cost of housing and food and the responsibilities of chores and upkeep out of necessity and also choice. These living arrangements provide financial benefits and also offer new ways to connect with others in community. For senior citizens, having a trusted younger adult share a space in their homes can provide a sense of connection, security, assistance with chores, and even financial support.

- ✓ **Bartering.** Bartering is a time-tested system of exchange in which goods and services are traded for other goods and services. Bartering systems were widely used in the past before they were largely replaced by today's monetary systems. Some communities or pockets of communities are enjoying a return to this kind of exchange that involves face-to-face interactions that help build connections and trust.

- ✓ **Gift Economy.** In a gift economy, goods and services are not traded or sold; instead, they are offered as a gift to the recipient, and the recipient determines the value of the gift. Gift economies are based on trust, gratitude, and generosity.

How willing are you to step outside your comfort zone and try out new ways of exchanging goods and services in community?

Practices for Connection: The Larger Community

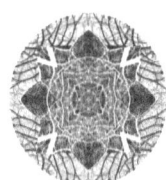

THIS CHAPTER OFFERS PRACTICES to ground you in your experience of larger community. Refer to these practices and the questions for deeper reflection as you continue to strengthen your connection to community in the coming months and years. Begin right where you are, with your local community.

Connecting to Community

Take a few minutes to reflect on your current level of engagement in your community. How does it feel? Are you as involved as you would like to be? Here are a few simple ways to improve your connection to community.

- ✓ **Your 21-Day Connection Plan**. On a piece of paper or in a document on your computer, list three actions you can take to make new connections in your local community. Take action on idea number one within the next seven days. Take action on idea number two within the following seven days, and idea number three within seven days after that. At the end of 21 days, reflect on and journal about your 21-Day Connection Plan. How was the experience for you? How has your level of connection with your community changed?

- ✓ **Connect with A Smile!** The next time you go out to the grocery store, make a conscious effort to smile at the people you meet. Notice the connections you make with others when you offer the gift of a smile. What feelings arise for you as you consciously engage with a smile?

- ✓ **Your Vision of Ideal Community**. Choose to do this activity when you have at least 20 minutes to be alone. Get still and quiet. You will need a writing instrument and journal or other paper for this activity.

- Sit or lie in a comfortable position with your eyes closed or gazing downward. With your body comfortable and relaxed, notice your breath as you inhale and exhale. Notice the cool air in your nostrils as you inhale. Feel the warmth of your breath in your nostrils as you exhale. Continue to notice your breathing for a few full breaths. Noticing your breath centers you in the present moment.

- Think about the ways you are connected and engaged in community. As you hold these connections in your mind, notice what feelings arise. Hold this awareness for a few minutes.

- Now, envision what your life would look like if you were engaged in your community at the level that you wish for. Imagine yourself connecting in all the ways that would make your life more satisfying and meaningful. Hold that vision in your imagination. What feelings are coming up for you? What are you noticing in your body? There is no need to change any of the feelings or sensations that you are experiencing. Simply notice them. Spend at least 10 minutes envisioning your ideal connection experience.

- Now return your awareness to your breathing. Notice your breath for a few minutes, then allow your breath to resume its natural rhythm for a few more breaths. Slowly open your eyes and bring your attention back to your surroundings.

- Using your journal and writing instrument, write about your ideal vision for connection in your community. Describe your vision of connection. In your vision how did you see yourself connected to your community? What insights or ideas came up for you? What feelings came up for you as you envisioned a state of ideal community?

Gratitude for Community

Make an intentional visit to a part of your community where people naturally gather. This may be a public park, town square, neighborhood cafe, or another area where you can observe and reflect. For this activity, bring a journal and writing instrument. After you arrive at your chosen neighborhood destination, find a comfortable place to sit where you can observe the surrounding people and activities.

Spend at least 20 minutes simply observing what you see in this small container of your community. Greet others with a smile. It's ok if someone starts a conversation with you. After all, this activity is about connection and puts you in the middle of community where connection happens. Once you have observed and possibly engaged with others, spend some time journaling about your experience with special focus on what you observed and what it is about your community for which you feel grateful. What insights or feelings came up for you in your experience in community?

21 Questions for Deeper Reflection

1. What is my sense of "belonging" in my community?
2. Am I connected in ways that make me feel that I am a valued contributor to my community?
3. How can I make a meaningful difference in my community?
4. What personal talents, skills, experience can I offer to enrich my community?
5. What are my personal motivations for engagement in my community?
6. What is one thing I can do to help build bridges of connection between teens and seniors in my community?
7. What personal barriers or obstacles are preventing me from expanding my engagement in my community?
8. How can I overcome the barriers that are limiting my community engagement?
9. What are three new ways I can connect with my community this year?
10. What is my ideal level of engagement in my community?
11. How satisfied am I with my current level of engagement in my community?
12. What is one volunteer opportunity I am willing to explore in my community?
13. What are three ways I can be a better neighbor in my immediate neighborhood?
14. How willing am I to commit to being a better neighbor?
15. How can I become more engaged in a community cause or issue that I care deeply about?

16. On a scale of 1-5, with 1 being low engagement and 5 being high engagement, how would I rate my level of engagement in my community?
17. What are some ways I can support local farmers and businesses in my community?
18. What is one action I can take to connect to an elderly person in my community?
19. How can I use the power of my smile to brighten someone's day today?
20. How can I express gratitude for the connections I have cultivated in my larger community?
21. How willing am I to reach out to offer help to a community member who has experienced a personal loss or tragedy?

4

Nature
Pathways to Connection

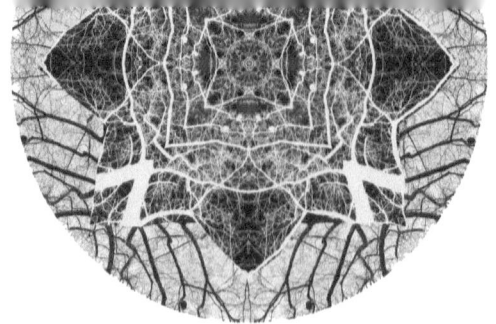

> Perhaps a new revelatory experience is taking place, an experience wherein human consciousness awakens to the grandeur and sacred quality of the Earth process. Humanity has seldom participated in such a vision since shamanic times, but in such a renewal lies our hope for the future for ourselves and for the entire planet on which we live.
>
> Thomas Berry

Connecting with the Heart of Nature

ALONG THE SPIRAL PATH with its five connection pathways to a deepening sense of community and belonging, the fourth pathway offers a reconnection to nature. Your relationship with nature reveals much about your relationship with yourself, because your connection to your True Self is mirrored in all other relationships. When you are self-aware, seeing with the eyes of the True Self, you see the world as whole and integrated. You see yourself as connected to all living things.

We must accept, embrace, and integrate all the aspects of who we are into our conscious awareness so we can experience life through the wholeness that is ours already. Then we can live and express in the experience of wholeness with the world. As your authentic self, you may notice that you yearn for more time in nature. You may notice that when you are in nature you experience an indescribable feeling of wholeness and peace. Though you may not always be close to a forest or cascading waterfall, you can still connect with nature just by looking at a tree, touching the ground with your bare feet, or listening to a bird singing.

Nature is vast and magnificent, yet so very close and intimate. We are of it, and it is of us. The simple remembrance of our intimacy with nature can bring us comfort and serenity. Right now, in this moment, you can open your heart to the nature of our world and see yourself as an integral part of the living system of earth.

How connected you feel to *you* directly impacts how you view the world around you. As you connect more deeply with your True Self, you live in the experience of your wholeness. Consciously connecting with the natural world reminds you of this wholeness.

> We feel whole and complete in nature. Spending time in nature connects us to the heart of who we really are.

When we are in nature, we experience our inner wholeness and see it expanded into the larger world. Our connection with nature is at the depth of who we really are. While those who are consciously aware of their connection to the natural world easily feel at home in nature, those who are not as aware of their connection to nature are equally transformed by the beauty and magnificence of the natural world as they experience it. This tells us that simply being in nature can be a transformational experience.

In the heart of nature, our hearts are opened. We bear witness with reverence to the sacredness of all. Your experience of nature helps to bring you into remembrance of your wholeness within.

When you connect to the natural world, you will feel a deep sense of belonging. Once you experience one of these transformational moments in the heart of nature, you will notice a deep longing to return to it wherever you are. It is in this sense of belonging to the natural world that we come into fuller experience of True Community.

Recognizing the Mindset of Separation

When was the last time you spent time in nature? With our busy lifestyles, many find it hard to set aside the time to be in nature, yet nature is all around us. We are in it at all times, because we are of nature and so never separate from it.

Yet many people see nature as separate from themselves. Those who see themselves as separate are likely to experience the world from a place of fear, lack, and distrust. They may think they have to compete with fierce independence to make it in the world. This mindset originates from a disconnection from the essence of their true selves and colors how these individuals experience the world they live in.

When you see yourself as separate from the natural world, you may feel a need to dominate and control in order to have enough for yourself and those you consider valuable or wish to protect—the few people you do not see as separate from you. Internally, those who see the world in this way are cut off from their true essence of love and peace. Rather than relating to themselves, others, and the natural world from a place of expanding inner love, their relationships are based in fear and contraction.

This mindset of separation from self, others, and nature is at the root of the ecological crisis we are experiencing in our world today. Those who see themselves as separate tend not to recognize or honor the sacred nature and intrinsic value of the earth, its inhabitants, and its resources. They see anyone or anything outside themselves as "other" than themselves. Seeing the earth as "other" makes it easier to justify the unbridled use of earth's precious natural resources without consideration of any negative consequences for present or future generations.

Choosing the Mindset of Connection

While the mindset of separation results in a sense of isolation and disconnection from self and the outer world, including nature, increasing numbers of people see the world as one of wholeness and connection. They experience the world through the mindset of connection and oneness. Because of a deep self-awareness, these individuals see themselves as an integral part of the natural world. They view their relationship with nature as one of living *with* nature in a state of inter-being, seeing themselves and all of humanity as connected and one with the natural world. They live life through the experience of the True Self.

When you experience the world through the expansive mindset of oneness and connection, you embrace all of nature, including humanity, and see it as sacred. You recognize the intrinsic value in all. You are connected to all through the great power of love, and your love for self expands to include all. You realize that you have a responsibility to care for and protect nature, because you see the earth as your home.

When you are one with nature, you desire to come together with others and with all the earth in peace and harmony. You care for the earth and all its inhabitants. You live in the awareness that nothing can separate you from your connection with the world. You realize that it is only limiting thoughts that can cause you to think you are separate.

Seeing Earth as Mother

Since ancient times many have felt a strong maternal connection with the earth. Seen from this perspective, the earth is like a tender and loving mother holding us in her loving care, feeding us, sheltering us, providing for our every need. And, like a loving mother, she loves us unconditionally. At home with earth, our loving mother, we experience the wholeness and unity of who we really are. We feel safe and held in the arms of love. We see the mother's loving gaze upon us and we gaze back into her loving eyes, our hearts connected as one.

For some, seeing the earth as a whole and living system helps to bring them into a closer sense of connection with it. Seeing the earth as a living being makes it easier to open our hearts in compassion and love, and spending time in nature connects us to the heart of who we really are. This way of seeing leads to a deepened desire to care for and nurture the planet that is our home.

Pause for a few minutes right now to try on this perspective of a maternal earth. How would your relationship with the natural world change if you viewed the earth as a loving mother?

Awe and Wonder in the Presence of Nature

When we make the time to connect with the natural world, it is as if we are joined, heart to heart, whole in the great love that connects us all. Seeing ourselves as one with nature, we live in the mystery that is life. Because we live in the mystery, we may experience times of awe and wonder at the unknowable vastness and magnificence that is our universe. We begin to understand that we are integrally connected to all living things.

In these moments, we also realize we are connected to something much bigger than ourselves. Rather than shrink in fear of it, we open ourselves to marvel at it in wonder and curiosity. We feel it is by grace that we are present to witness and participate in such wonders.

When you think of experiencing awe and wonder in nature, you may bring to mind spectacular and breathtaking aspects of nature; however, we can experience awe and wonder in the smallest, seemingly mundane aspects of nature. It is really a matter of our putting these in the context of the whole and unimaginably vast universe that we live in. There is not any surefire way to predict what will elicit that sense of awe and wonder for you. By being fully present you open yourself to be with the experience as you witness it.

Here are some simple ideas you can try that can help connect you to a sense of awe and wonder at the natural world:

- looking up at the starry night sky on a clear night
- watching baby animals at play
- watching waves crash on a beach
- watching a cascading waterfall
- watching a sunset or sunrise
- watching a bee gathering pollen from a flower
- witnessing a thunderstorm on a summer night

Finding Community and Purpose through Nature

Because our connection with nature brings us into greater sense of alignment and wholeness within, it naturally helps us cultivate a deeper sense of community and purpose in our lives. Being in nature might not seem like the most obvious place to begin when you want to experience a greater sense of community, but more and more the evidence shows that connection to the natural world has a multitude of benefits that support overall well-being and a greater sense of belonging. From forest bathing to adopting an environmentally friendly lifestyle, from taking a walk in the woods to adventure challenges, there are activities in nature to suit every personality type.

Taking time for simple actions such as self-reflection in nature has been shown to connect us more quickly and more powerfully to our innate wisdom. This, in turn, leads to an increase in creative solutions and practical steps that improve the environment, beginning in our own community. This is the path that has guided and continues to guide indigenous peoples to care for the earth, which many cultures have long associated with the mother. This perspective is now shared by growing numbers of people who are beginning to realize that their relationship with themselves is reflected in their relationships in the outer world. This includes their relationship to the world of nature.

Benefits to Health and Well-Being

How do you feel when you are in nature? The next time you are in a forest, a park, or another natural setting, pause for a few minutes. Notice what you are feeling in your body. Do you feel energized? Peaceful? Happy? Calm? Grateful? Uplifted? Becoming more mindful of how you feel when you are immersed in nature deepens your self-awareness and enhances your experience of connecting through nature.

While we can experience within ourselves how nature makes us feel, we are coming to understand from scientific studies and research that spending time in nature is far more than just an enjoyable or pleasant experience. Connecting with nature has many positive benefits for our health and well-being. While an in-depth review of the studies are outside the scope and purpose of this book, you may wish to deepen your own understanding of these benefits by exploring some of the studies that demonstrate the health benefits of a connection to and immersion in the natural world.

Nature's benefits to our health and well-being include an increase of our experience of peace and happiness, feeling more empowered, reduced stress, improved nervous system functioning, and an enhanced ability to fight diseases. When you are in nature you may have noticed subtle (and sometimes not-so-subtle) shifts in your feeling state, your energy level, or your ability to focus and concentrate. Or you may not have noticed any changes at all. We are learning that time spent in nature is beneficial, whether or not we notice it at the time.

Our Responsibility to the Earth

As we come into deeper awareness of our connection to the earth and the gifts of the natural world, our hearts open in love. Immersed in nature, we open our awareness to the gracious gifts that nature continually gives. The giving earth is our home. It is the place where we experience a deep sense of true belonging. Our hearts beat in resonance with the heart of the earth when we see it as a living system that sustains us. As we receive with open hearts the bountiful gifts of the earth, we naturally want to give back. We begin to participate in the natural flow of the life. We understand that we are stewards of the natural world, nurturing and caring for it even as we enjoy its gifts.

When we are disconnected from nature, we feel emptiness and longing. We sense that something vital is missing from our lives. That something we are missing is the awareness of our lifeline of connection to nature that sustains us and reminds us of our innate wholeness. We have been given the gift of life on earth, our home to live in and care for while we live briefly on this planet. Our stewardship responsibilities invite us to consciously care for the earth, so that we and future generations can enjoy the beauty and bounty of our earth home.

When we enter into True Community, we look for ways we can fulfill our responsibilities as earth stewards because we understand the practical need for people to work together on common goals and needs. Our felt responsibility to care for the natural world can work to bring us together in community with others who share our sense of responsibility to take care of the earth. Such coming together with shared goals for the care of the earth is another way our connection with nature brings us into experience of True Community.

Connecting with the Wisdom of the Earth

The natural world is a great and wise teacher. We can learn much if we pause to listen deeply and intently. In truth, the earth continually offers its wisdom whether or not we choose to listen. The lessons we can learn are vast: unconditional love, resilience, harmony, balance, self-regulation, and so much more.

Our earth home holds the collected wisdom of its more than four billion years existence. We are of the earth, and so we too hold that wisdom within our deepest selves if we but learn to trust it and tap into it. When you are guided by your inner wise self, you in essence are accessing the deep wisdom of the earth. In nature we can discover and observe wondrous repeating patterns that remind us of the intricacy and complexity of life and also of the basic and unifying patterns from which the natural world unfolds. Nature reminds us that, even in seeming chaos, it self-regulates into balance and harmony so that its ecosystems can thrive.

From the wisdom of nature, we can learn so much about ourselves, and we can deepen our experiences of self in relationship with our external world. For example, a tree, grounded deeply and securely into the earth by its roots, is able to withstand the winds that arise. Firm in its grounding, its branches can sway freely in the wind, expressing fully its "tree-ness" in the world. Acorns hold within themselves the potential for their full expression into majestic oak trees. Seeds are imprinted to become plants that feed and nourish.

How can you apply nature's wisdom to inform and heighten your experience of True Community? If there is potentiality in every aspect of nature, what possibilities might you hold for unfolding to your full and potent expression in the world?

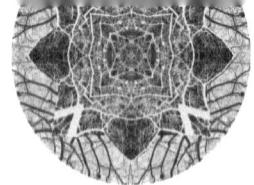

> Human use, population, and technology have reached that certain stage where mother Earth no longer accepts our presence with silence.
> The Dalai Lama

Going Deeper: Nature and Community

WHEN WE CONNECT WITH NATURE, our connection with our authentic selves is deepened, leading to a fuller and more expansive experience of True Community both within and without. The way in which we show up in the world is greatly influenced by the way we view the world and our relationship with it. When we see ourselves as one with the natural world, we see and treat the world with love and compassion.

However, if we objectify the world and see ourselves as somehow separate from it, the ways we treat the natural world, and ourselves, will be very different. When this is the case, our tendency is to treat the natural world as a commodity to be used and exploited. Every day we see more and more evidence of our perceived disconnection from nature. Rising temperatures, wildfires, dependence on fossil fuels, and the extinction of entire species are just some of the messages the earth is sending that something has gone terribly wrong. That something is in large part our forgetfulness of our wholeness and connection with the natural world.

Have we lost our way forward? How did we get so off-track? Disconnection from our true nature leads us astray from our truth of wholeness and alignment. When we are disconnected from nature, we are in essence disconnected from ourselves, and we may feel this as a kind of indescribable emptiness or loss.

To lose oneself is to lose one's sense of wholeness and happiness. Disconnection leads to feelings of fear, isolation, loneliness, and lack. It leads to disharmony and violence resulting from the absence of love and compassion toward ourselves, each other, and to the earth. In fear and distrust, we isolate ourselves from community.

Is a brighter future possible? This chapter will take a deeper look at how our forgetfulness and a mindset of separation affect the natural world. It will offer ways to bring yourself back into alignment with a deeper experience of True Community through which a more beautiful world is possible.

Focus Questions: *Nature*

Reflect on the following focus questions to return to the experience of True Community through your connection to nature. In your journal, write down your responses to the following three questions:

1. At this point in my life, how would I describe my connection to nature?
2. How committed am I to going deeper on my pathway to connection with nature?
3. True connection with nature begins within. How would I assess my connection to my inner self right now?

Earth's Clarion Cry for Help

A whale, full of plastics, washes up on the beach. Icebergs crash into the sea. Sea levels rise. Entire ecosystems are degraded, and rivers and streams polluted. Endangered species disappear and become extinct. The incidence of wildfires increases.

The earth is in trouble—deep trouble.

It is becoming increasingly clear that the common denominator in our ecological crisis is the human factor. The devastating effects of human actions on the earth are visible all around us, and conditions worsen by the day. How did it come to this? How can we best respond to the alarming destruction of the natural world happening all around us?

The good news is that we are beginning to wake up to the clarion call the earth is sending forth. Alarmed at what they see happening around them, many are taking impassioned action. Many individuals, families, and groups are taking decisive action to reverse the damage while there is still time. We are all needed, and there are practical ways to make a difference now, beginning right in our local communities.

A Dangerous Narrative

In the high-stakes and often divisive environment in our world, some individuals and groups are speaking up and speaking out against who and what they blame as the root cause of the decimation of our natural world. Driven by legitimate concerns and a deep love for our dwindling natural resources, theirs is an epic narrative of "good" versus "bad" in which they see themselves positioned against those they hold responsible for the environmental crisis.

This approach, while well-intentioned, can all too often perpetuate "otherness," a condition that pits "us" against "them" and further divides rather than brings the community together around a common goal. This long-running narrative of disconnection has, in truth, led us to the desperate place we find ourselves in today. When we recognize approaches that are not working to unify us, we become increasingly confident that our efforts are making and will continue to make a real difference, leading us into a deeper experience of community even as we take corrective action and seek to create a better world for all.

When any of us chooses to move into action, speak out about, or work on behalf of the environment, we can first take into consideration the hallmarks of a narrative that is both divisive and dangerous. Such a narrative:

- Views humanity as separate from nature
- Sees nature's resources as commodities to be exploited
- Begins with blame
- Breaks down in a stalemate between opposing parties

A Fresh Narrative for Collective Action

Other groups and individuals, also concerned about the state of the environment, are choosing a fresh narrative. Just as concerned about the state of our world, theirs is a story of hope and possibility, of connection and collaboration, of inclusion and diversity. The focus of their conversation is one that begins with common concerns and a willingness to begin where we are, without need for assigning blame or beginning with a fixed position.

This narrative does not replace the less helpful narrative described above. Instead, it builds on the lessons learned from it. It is a story large enough to support the flourishing of all life. This fresh approach to the environmental crisis at hand is, at its heart, about relationship.

Though it seems new, it is the narrative begun by indigenous peoples who hold our natural world and humanity as precious and sacred. In this more expansive and inclusive story, we open our hearts and minds to all humans as co-creators of our future. This new story reminds us that we are in this together. As Ram Dass aptly says, "We're all just walking each other home."

Here are the hallmarks of this more open and collaborative approach:

- Emphasizes participating *with* the environment rather than seeking to dominate or control it
- Focuses on healing and regeneration
- Begins with a view of all things as sacred
- Brings people together

The earth is in trouble. There is no question about that. Our earth home has given and given to us; now, her resources are becoming depleted in our frenzied quest for more and more. She has sounded a call for help, and it is up to each one of us to find aligned ways to heed and answer that call. It is our collective response, made up of our many individual choices, that will determine whether we come together as community to rally around and protect what we hold most dear and how well we do that.

What actions are you, your family, your neighborhood, and your business taking to make a difference? What are some of the quickest and easiest ways to take positive steps to create a better environment?

A Better Environment Begins Close to Home

The answer is closer than you think. The future of our world and its inhabitants brightens as we deepen our awareness and connection to our inner selves. Taking the time to connect with your heart's wisdom empowers citizens of every age to right action. Though our path to that action may vary, it always begins within.

You can connect with your heart's wisdom when you slow down and listen to your inner guidance. Some refer to this inner guidance as the still small voice within. Many use periods of reflection, contemplation, mediation, and prayer to connect them with their inner selves. Connection with nature is another powerful way to move us into the space of the heart's wisdom, where we can access our creativity to come up with innovative ideas and solutions to even the most challenging and complex circumstances. Learning to love the natural world as an extension of ourselves is the only sustainable way to nurture and regenerate the natural world.

Meeting Yourself Where You Are

The complex and dynamic environmental challenges we face today require us to meet ourselves and each other where we are. We must come to accept ourselves, flaws and all, and to cultivate self-compassion. As our capacity for self-compassion expands, so too does our ability to have a positive impact on the world around us, including nature. We can no longer afford to bury our heads in the sand or resort to denial about the challenges we are facing. We can no longer perpetuate an "other-ness" mindset or see ourselves as separate from one another or the natural world.

Decisive, discerning action is an imperative. There is no other way. The way forward begins with self-acceptance, and then we must accept where we are from a larger environmental perspective. We must see, understand, and acknowledge our own actions—

actions which have in some cases inflicted damage on our local and global environments. By meeting ourselves where we are, we can see our way forward to a better world for ourselves and for future generations. The solutions lie not in blaming and finger-pointing, but in accountability, responsibility, and action.

Local Action for a More Beautiful World

There's no doubt, the need is urgent. Clearly, we must work together to take positive and collective action that will support the healing and regeneration of the planet and its ecosystems. But where can we start? And how?

Around the world, people are becoming more conscious and more aware of their impact on their environment. People of all ages are eager to learn about actions they can take at the local level that will result in the regeneration, renewal, and revitalization of our world. In your local community, you can take action to create a more beautiful world by coming together with others to share ideas.

"We cannot solve problems by using the same kind of thinking we used when we created them," Albert Einstein once said. Reversing the catastrophic impact of human actions born of greed and complacency requires a completely new mindset and a fresh approach. Now is the time to identify new ways to regenerate and restore the health and vitality of natural systems, and it is imperative that we find new ways of doing so.

Taking Action as a Community

Communities across the country are meeting success with a heart-based approach that begins with wholeness and interconnection. A more beautiful world *is* possible. It begins within each one of us. Here are two ideas for community actions that bring people together to share ideas about ways to address environmental issues:

1. **Coordinate a Community Conversation.** Discuss simple actions anyone can take at the local level. Partner with a local community group other organization to host a free

public event to discuss simple actions to preserve and nurture the earth, beginning locally.

2. **Show a Documentary or Educational Film.** Gather at your local library or another public meeting space to educate members of your community about current and potential environmental issues. Host a conversation that explores actions some communities are taking to address these pressing environmental concerns. Follow up with a candid group discussion of ideas for local action.

Individual Action and Advocacy

What is your response to the call of the earth? How will you step forward to lend a hand? What actions can you take for a more beautiful world? How could your willingness to take actions that address environmental issues bring meaning and purpose to your life?

When we live in the awareness of our inner truth, we naturally embrace all the world in our desire for a more hopeful future. The clean air we desire for ourselves and our children, we likewise desire for all people and all the earth. We want to clean up the plastic tainted oceans, not just for ourselves but for the health and well-being of the entire planet and all its inhabitants. We advocate for fresh clean drinking water for all and become more conscious of how wasteful habits harm the environment. We seek to shift to more environmentally friendly practices that benefit not only our family and friends but the entire earth.

What benefits one benefits all. Our individual realignment with inner truth leads us to take actions that improve our common experience of life on earth. When we know who we truly are as one with all creation, we seek to lift humanity and the earth up to the natural beauty, magnificence, and potential we now see in ourselves and others. We understand that we are all connected integrally to the world we live in.

This understanding emerges naturally as we connect with our True Selves and express authentically in the world. This is our innate and original understanding. We have simply forgotten it in the course of our lived experiences in the world. A sustainable and beautiful world begins within each of us. Guided by our inner wisdom and with the support of community, we can begin to take a more empowered and proactive approach to living in harmony with the earth. Standing resolute in our power, we can take a strong stand for the earth.

There is always hope for a better future. Hope inspires us to creative action, individually and collectively, on behalf of nature and the natural world. When we have hope about our relationship to nature, we can more readily draw upon our inner resources of wisdom, resilience, and creativity to reconnect with the natural world and more readily see how it leads us back to ourselves and the full experience of community.

Having endured and risen up from the adversity and challenges of the past, we can draw upon lessons learned. We can return to True Community and the truth that lies within us to guide us forward to a better world for all.

Practices for Connection: Nature

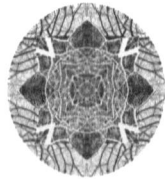

THIS CHAPTER OFFERS SIMPLE PRACTICES to ground you in your experience of nature. Refer to these practices and questions for deeper reflection again and again as you strengthen your connection to nature and the natural world in the coming months and years.

Experiencing Nature

In our busy lives it is easy to get caught up in our day-to-day routines that often can be stressful and hectic. We may think we do not have extra time to get outdoors in nature. When this thought comes into your mind, it may help to remember that nature is all around us. We are immersed in it, and we are of it.

Still, actually going out into the natural world with the conscious intent to connect with nature brings you into a deeper awareness of your connection to nature. Following are simple practices to ground you in the experience of nature:

- ✓ **Take a Nature Walk.** Look for opportunities to join a group for a nature walk, a walking meditation, or a forest bathing experience. These activities facilitated by an experienced meditation leader can take you on a meaningful experience of presence in and to nature. The experience of consciously connecting with nature while in the company of others further amplifies your experience.

    If participating in a group walk is not feasible, take a solo walk. No training or experience is necessary! As you walk, simply notice what is happening around you in the natural world. Besides noticing the activity of wildlife, observe seemingly inanimate and foundational elements of nature, such as the rocks, tree bark, and fallen leaves. Simply notice the minute components of the natural world, such as lichen growing on rocks. Be aware of any feelings that arise within you and how you feel about yourself and your connection to nature.

- ✓ **Sensing Nature.** This simple activity can bring you into mindful awareness of nature by engaging your five senses. You can try this activity anytime you are out in nature, whether in your backyard, in a park, or in a forest. Bring your awareness to your surroundings. Notice what you see with your eyes. Next, notice the sounds you hear from the natural world. Do you hear birds singing? Leaves rustling in the breeze? What do you smell or taste? How does your body feel when the sun shines down or the cool breeze blows? Simply enjoy taking in the sights and sounds of nature, appreciating how you experience the natural world through your senses.

- ✓ **Photographing Nature.** Photographing nature helps us see it through new eyes. Take a nature walk with a camera. Or use your cell phone camera. Set out with the intention to capture images from the natural world. Look for elements of nature that you might otherwise overlook. Notice textures, such as the bark on trees, veins in leaves, or dry leaves on the ground. Notice insects, rocks, and other elements to which you are drawn. Print and frame your photographs to decorate your living space or for meditative purposes—or use your printed photos in collages or other art creations.

- ✓ **Create a Nature Mandala.** The word *mandala* comes from the Sanskrit language and refers to a circle or center. The mandala represents wholeness. Mandalas consist of integrated elements radiating out around a unifying center. You can create a mandala from natural materials gathered from your own backyard or any place you encounter the natural world. To create a mandala from natural objects, simply choose natural elements to which you are drawn, such as rocks, leaves, sticks, seeds, pinecones, mosses, berries, sand, and acorns. Choose an object or objects for the center of your mandala. Place the other gathered objects around the center. Or, you may choose to create a circular shape first and then fill it in from the outside edges moving inward to the center.

After the mandala feels complete, spend some time contemplating its beauty and wholeness. Notice any feelings that come up for you. Besides connecting us with nature in a creative way, making a mandala is a lesson in non-attachment. The activity is about the creative journey or process of creating the mandala, meditating upon it, and then leaving it in its natural setting where is will eventually be re-dispersed into the natural world from which it originated. Taking a photo of your mandala allows you to capture the image to which you can return to for contemplative purposes or simply to recall the experience of creative expression.

✓ **Listening to Nature's Symphony.** This is a sensory activity that connects us deeply with nature through our sense of hearing. All you need do is go outdoors during the day or at night. Be sure to carry your journal along with a pen or pencil. Sit or lie in a comfortable, relaxed position with your eyes closed. Now simply listen to all the sounds of nature you hear around you. You may hear a cacophony of sound rising and falling. Or perhaps you will hear only faint and indecipherable whispers on the wind.

Notice the layers of sound, such as bursts of birdsongs interspersed over a background of cicadas, frogs, or the wind blowing through the trees. What do you hear? Notice the sounds that are loudest and then listen for the quieter sounds in the background. Spend at least 20 minutes just listening. Then write in your journal about the experience. Record any impressions or insights that arose. You may also choose to record the sounds using your cell phone recorder or other device. The point of this exercise, however, is the experience of connecting with nature through our sense of hearing, so be certain to stay attuned to all that is unfolding around you.

- ✓ **Honoring and Appreciating Wildlife.** Opening our hearts to wildlife can open our hearts to the larger world around us. We gain a deeper appreciation for the animals around us by observing them in their natural environment, by educating ourselves about them, and by treating them with love and respect. Putting out bird feeders in the months when natural food may be scarce can help nurture and strengthen the birds for their long migratory journeys. Find creative ways to learn about and open your heart to wildlife. See their lives as sacred as are all lives.

- ✓ **Planning for Green Space.** Conscious city/county planners include plans for green space and amenities such as walking and biking trails because they know the benefits of physical activity and spending leisure time in nature. While you may not hold a position as a community planner, you can take an active role in your community to advocate for green space and parks where community residents can spend more time outdoors. How does your neighborhood, city, or county incorporate green spaces and other outdoor spaces for physical and leisure activity? What actions can you take to speak out for more planned green space, hiking trails, and parks in our community?

- ✓ **Take a Nature Break.** Being present with nature brings you home to yourself. Pause indoor work tasks to take a brisk walk outside or simply to walk to a window and take in the view of the natural world. Even though you may live in a city paved in concrete, look out to see if you can see birds or trees through your window. Mobile devices and laptop computers and flexible work schedules now make it easier than ever to be mobile in our work. Work outside, pausing when possible to notice the natural world around you. If you must work inside, take breaks. Walk outside or simply look out a window to notice nature around you—trees, plants, flowers, and birds.

Inspiring Children to Connect With Nature

The future of the earth is our children and their children going forward; yet, hope for the future begins with us, here in the present, as we model to our children loving and responsible care for the earth. As our hearts open in loving care for our children and our earth home, we instill in them a hope for the future and a connection to the natural world. Children are eager and enthusiastic learners, and they will quickly pick up on the responsible actions you model that lead to full thriving and a sustainable future for all.

Here are some simple, responsible and fun actions you can take with children to remind them of their innate connection with nature.

- **Set a good example.** Actions such as recycling, turning off lights when not in use, turning off water when brushing teeth, and using re-usable bags for shopping model responsible, eco-friendly behaviors for children. Be sure to explain and remind children of why these actions are important to the entire planet. Having children assist with activities like recycling engages them in learning by doing with adult supervision where appropriate.

- **Love unconditionally.** Show unconditional love to your children and the natural world. Children who feel loved for who they are and are affirmed feel as if they really matter. This, in turn, strengthens their connection with themselves, others, and the world, to include their connection to nature. Model loving connection to the natural world so that children experience being *with* nature and do not feel separate from it.

- **Express wonder and awe.** Sharing special moments with children in which they can experience wonder in nature opens their eyes to the magnificence of the natural world.

Looking at the stars on a clear night, visiting a waterfall, or watching the sunset are some practical ways to connect children to the wonders of nature.

- **Visit a local farm.** Some farms welcome visits by individuals and families. Consider a trip to learn about life on the farm and perhaps enjoy natural foods from the garden. Interacting with farm animals can be educational and fun for all.

- **Take a nature walk.** Taking a walk in nature can be a natural learning experience for children. Encourage children to explore and discover by noticing the larger elements of nature, such as trees and ponds, as well as those elements that are easily overlooked, such as insects under a log, minnows in a stream, or veins on a leaf. Draw their attention to patterns in nature and the ways various elements and components of nature are interconnected in larger ecosystems.

- **Go camping.** A camping trip takes some planning and effort, but the opportunities to really connect with nature are worth it. If it is not feasible for you to go to a campground, plan a fun campout right in your backyard.

- **What do I see?** Engage children's creativity by having them lie on a blanket on the ground and look for shapes in the clouds. Notice hawks or other birds soaring in the air. Point out the beauty of trees against the sky. Invite children to look for other things in the sky.

- **Plant a garden.** A garden is a wonderful teacher. Engage children in the entire process from planning, planting, watering, weeding, and harvesting. And don't forget eating! Starting plants from seeds can add another layer of learning. Your enthusiasm will go a long way toward keeping children interested and excited as they connect with nature.

- **Express gratitude for the natural world.** You can continually model and teach gratitude as you point out beautiful elements of nature. Mention how the plants love the rain showers and how rain helps gardens and flowers grow. Take time on a nature walk or in your backyard. Invite your child to notice one thing in nature he or she is grateful for.

- **Teach farm-to-table concept.** This concept is enhanced by a trip to a farm, if possible, or by the experience of a backyard garden. As you eat a meal, open a conversation about the food on the table. Explain in simple terms the steps that produce takes as it moves from the farm to table.

- **Encourage outdoor play.** Spending more time outdoors benefits children's health and is a healthy alternative to screen time on electronic devices.

- **Have fun!**

21 Questions for Deeper Reflection

1. What steps can I take to improve self-care and self-value, which supports a reconnection to nature and True Community?
2. How will my choice to improve my relationship with my True Self contribute to a better environment?
3. What steps can I take to improve relationships with family members and close friends, which supports a reconnection to nature and True Community?
4. How will my choice to focus on my relationships with family and friends contribute to a better environment?
5. What steps can I take to improve my relationship with my local community, which supports a reconnection to nature and True Community?
6. How will my choice to get involved in my local community contribute to a better environment?
7. What steps can I take to improve my relationship with the natural world?
8. How will my deliberate connection with nature contribute to a better environment?
9. How might viewing earth as a mother change my relationship with nature?
10. How will my choice to engage consciously with communities to which I belong contribute to a better environment?
11. How can I take a proactive and powerful approach to living on the earth, guided by my inner wisdom and inner power?
12. What is one important lesson I have learned from nature? Or what is one gift that nature has given me?
13. What is one small action I can take today to nurture and protect our planet?

14. Our passion for protecting our natural world often is sparked by the happy childhood memories of time we spent in nature. Recalling these memories can reconnect us with the feelings and emotions of time spent in nature. What is one childhood memory I have of spending time enjoying nature? What feelings come up for me as I reflect on this memory? Find a way to express gratitude for this memory.

15. When I think about my child, grandchild, or other children I know, what kind of world does my heart desire for them?

16. What actions am I taking in my life now that contribute to a more beautiful world for future generations?

17. How can I inspire and instill respect and reverence for the earth in children today?

18. What are the lessons of the consequences of greed and "otherness"?

19. What does a world in which there is a reverence for the sacredness of our earth home look like? What qualities are present? How is this different from what I am currently experiencing or witnessing?

20. What can I learn from indigenous people about living in connection and community, not just with other humans but all of the natural world?

21. How committed or willing am I to engage in local efforts and events intended to raise awareness about environmental concerns?

5

The Global Community
Pathways to Connection

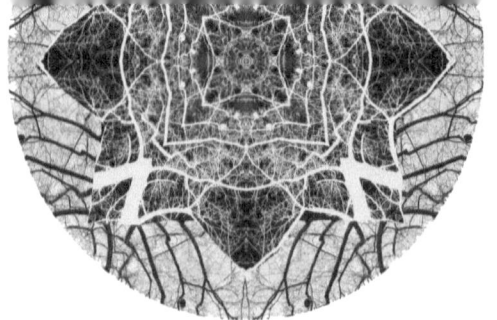

*I live my life in widening circles
that reach out across the world.*

Rainer Maria Rilke

Global Awareness

THE FIFTH PATHWAY ALONG The Spiral Path is that of global connection. When we choose this pathway, we experience an expanded sense of community and belonging that includes the entire world. These broader connections bring us into a fuller experience of True Community. They inform how we see the world—and ourselves. As we connect with people who may live at a great physical distance but with whom we share much, we widen the circle of awareness.

True Community includes connection to the world around us—not just our immediate environment but also a connection to the rich cultural diversity of our world and the gifts and challenges at play in distant lands. As we become aware of what is happening in the greater world, we often learn more about our own lives through both contrast and similarities. There are a variety of connections we can make to expand our awareness of what's happening globally, and we will explore some of these in a later chapter.

As with the previous pathways to community, we begin by adopting a state of being and with an awareness of the wholeness and connection that is our inner truth. At the individual level, community can be seen as the coming together in our awareness of all the perceived fragments or aspects of ourselves. Each piece or fragment is integral to the whole. From this realization of an inner community, we come to experience the world through a lens of welcome and wholeness and thus connect more easily to the world around us.

All external experience reflects the truth we hold within. When we allow wholeness within, we move into a realization of True Community through which we see and experience the world. It is through our outer experiences—including our relationships with family and friends, larger community, nature, and the greater world—that we connect more vitally and meaningfully. These connections enrich our experience of community, and deepening connections along each pathway support connection along the other pathways to True Community.

> Honesty, integrity, and compassion expressed uniquely into the world by individuals who see themselves as whole leads to the experience of True Community experienced by many across borders and the span of oceans.

Start with Heart

The experience of global community is made possible through self-love and trust at the individual level. Because our inner wholeness allows us to open ourselves to the full experience of connection to the greater world, global connection begins in the heart. Our connection to the world around us is expanded and enriched by a growing awareness of ourselves and the interconnected web of relationships that connects us to others.

As we make connections in the world, our natural impulse moves us toward greater and greater expansion. Part of the desire to know ourselves is spurred by an inner desire to understand how we fit into the larger context of the world. Our sense of belonging develops as we see more clearly how we fit into the larger community.

When we feel we belong, we see that we have value. We know we can contribute in meaningful ways. Then we can see there is purpose for our lives. That sense of purpose is interwoven into our sense of belonging when we realize that we are integral to our community and to the world.

When the desire to make a contribution arises, our natural curiosity leads us to learn about the world around us. We become curious about other parts of our world and those from cultures that differ vastly from our own, because we now feel a connection to those with whom we share this sacred earth. We become whole through our connection to the wholeness of the world. We see that all are integral to the whole and know that the whole has intrinsic value and so each aspect holds that same intrinsic value. All are needed for wholeness to be experienced, and this awareness leads us to great compassion and interest.

Learning About the World and Ourselves

Our innate curiosity and yearning to experience the world inspire us to want to learn more about the world. This process of discovery brings us greater knowledge about the world, its people, and their cultures. We are in effect broadening our global awareness as we explore and learn about the world. This awareness facilitates our willingness to make connections with others in the world.

In turn, this expands our understanding of who we are and how we fit into the world. When we take the time to demonstrate interest in other cultures and global events, we are increasing our capacity for compassion as well as our competence in contributing in meaningful ways to meet global needs. As we follow the desire to learn more and more about the world, we deepen our understanding of other cultures and the traditions and values of ethnic groups and those who come from other regions and countries.

Our knowledge and awareness of global happenings impact the world in positive ways. Knowing more about the world opens us to a broader view of the world and introduces us to new possibilities and new ways of seeing current and historic events. When we see the world only from our own perspective, our view is limited by our mindset and experience. A commitment to consciously connect with the concerns of others who hail from different backgrounds paves the way for greater peace and prosperity.

Global connections afford us the opportunity to cultivate compassion and empathy. When we are more connected at this level, we set the stage for dialogue and understanding. A more peaceful world becomes possible as we begin to expand our consciousness to include and embrace people and concerns that are global in scope and perspective.

Connecting Across Differences

At our most basic levels, we are connected with every other human on earth because we all belong to one humanity. When we come to realize and understand that on some level we are all connected, we cultivate a sense of compassion for ourselves and others. This compassion and common understanding support even greater connection which lead to a more fulfilling experience of life on an individual and collective level.

All humans have basic needs. These include food and water, sleep and warmth, safety and security, love and belonging. By nature, we are social beings who live in relationship with one another. We are better able to get our needs met through our social relationships; in fact, we thrive best in community. Because we need each other, we connect in relationship. From those connections, communities emerge and in those communities we are given the opportunity to grow and thrive.

The compassion born of this realization of oneness with humanity contributes to a more consciously connected world. Even though we may seem more different than we are alike in terms of appearance, customs, language, and dress, we can find comfort in knowing that we are connected in oneness in our common humanity. The pathway of global connection leads us to focus more and more on what unites us, rather than what divides or separates us.

Ways the World Connects

While we are innately connected at that deeper level of our common humanity, our social and economic connections have developed slowly over time. These connections were formed in many ways, including through the early migrations of groups who moved from place to place in search of food and shelter. Cultures also came into closer contact through travel along early trade routes.

Early explorations to discover new lands led to connections and encounters. While these sometimes led to clashes, exploitation, and even the assimilation of others for purposes of domination and control, they also introduced new ideas. More recently, leaps in scientific and technological understanding and discoveries have come forth from such connections and, in turn, have connected the world as never before.

The world of today would hardly seem possible or recognizable to people living just one hundred years ago. Here are some examples of ways the world is becoming more and more connected.

Technology. Advances in technology are happening at a dizzying pace at points all around the globe. The world of technology is changing all aspects of our lives and how we connect with each other. Our world now depends on technology, and the benefit of that technology is the ease and affordability of connection with others around the world.

Communications. Today we can communicate almost instantly with other people living on the other side of the world through communication technology, including cell phones, social media, and video-conferencing. Businesses, governments, and other organizations can hold meetings and make important decisions by electronic technology. The ability to communicate on-demand and instantaneously reduces travel and transportation costs. It also saves energy by eliminating the need for air travel for meetings and other purposes. Communication is vital for our living in community and for connecting with other communities both locally and worldwide.

Trade. The world is connected through trade. While trading has connected people from distant lands for centuries, the trade routes of the past have given way to much faster modes of moving products from manufacturer to consumer. Global trade connects the world. Businesses and nations are connected by trade agreements, and global trade has helped to usher in the global economy.

Travel. The world seems to shrink as our ability to travel great distances in shorter and shorter periods of time increases. Our airspace is now filled with large airplanes transporting people, goods, and services across the globe at faster speeds.

Governments. More than ever governments around the world are connected by agreements, treaties, and other formal connections. Economic connections among nations and between businesses large and small have led to a global economy and greater engagement between world governments.

Thoughts on Economic Globalization

When we talk about globalization, many people immediately think of economic globalization. We live and interact in a world that is connected and defined largely through the lens of economics. In many ways, we live within and under the influence of a global economy. Economic globalization has connected citizens of the world in many ways; yet, those connections are largely based on transactional relationships often motivated by the drive for greater and greater business profits.

The large businesses, nations, and others that drive the global economy see a perceived need for accelerated and unimpeded growth. This is an approach often rooted in the mindset of fear and lack. Competition, driven by greed for more and more, is a hallmark of this mindset. While connections and relationships are considered important, the underlying motivation of such players on the world stage is often to use social connections primarily to drive favorable economic transactions.

While there are some side benefits of economic globalization, by and large these transactions lack the heart-full approach of social connections created and sustained through human social interactions and choices that seek to unite people in peaceful, compassionate connection for the greater good of humanity. While the frenzied quest to dominate for economic gain is a common motivator, there is a growing awareness that this approach cannot continue unchecked.

More and more of us realize that Earth's precious and limited resources are becoming depleted at alarming rates. There is an increasing understanding that we all suffer as global temperatures rise. Many see that the continued dependence on fossil fuels cannot go on unabated. The decimation of the earth through fracking, deforestation, and other greedy practices will only speed up the destruction of the world we call home.

As our world becomes more connected through globalized markets, communication and travel, it is increasingly important that we treat each other with respect, integrity, and honesty. Schools and businesses are responding to the quickening pace of globalization by developing curriculums and training programs to prepare students and the workforce for engaging and living in a global environment. Many business leaders are waking up and leading conversation and movement toward more conscious business practices, based in the experience of True Community.

Many local communities are exploring ways to live with the earth rather than seeking to control and dominate it or ravaging its raw products for financial gain and control. They are seeking to put heart and compassion back into business, beginning locally and spreading globally. For example, fair trade practices work in cooperation with native workers and artisans so these craftspeople can sell their own products in a fair and equitable global market.

Rather than resorting to the inhumane practice of using indigenous peoples for cheap labor in factories, people around the globe are choosing to form independent and interconnected businesses. These innovative companies are producing goods that are valued for the quality, beauty, and value they bring to consumers and to the world. Fair trade practices are built on trust and integrity. They naturally promote healthy and heartfelt connections among people who care for each other and seek a return to the human element in the world of trade. Such practices return dignity and purpose to those who have suffered from the indignities that stem from greed and the desire for greater economic power.

While we may disagree with business leaders and those from the economic world who are steeped in a less equitable experience of the global economy, their business acuity and acumen, business skills, and experiences are important. We can learn from the past and allow it to inform a growing desire to do things differently. Business leaders who open their hearts and minds to new possibilities can help lead the way to new ways of doing business in the world.

The Effects of Globalization

While our understanding of the world and how it works has led to unparalleled and advantageous discoveries and advances that contribute to our global connection, that same process has also had negative consequences that can no longer be overlooked. In essence, there is both an upside and a downside to globalization from an economic perspective. Let's take a closer look at both sides of the picture.

The Upside of Globalization

Globalization has brought nations together in mutually beneficial relationships. The nature of these many varied relationships is often to support global trade initiatives. These global arrangements tend to be driven by economic concerns. Other relationships involve various treaties and agreements that outline conditions for working together toward common goals, such as trade, social issues, peace negotiations, or world health issues.

The basis of a more peaceful and just world is our ability to understand others and find common ground. Nations that come together around common goals strengthen connections in the global environment through greater understanding and a shared purpose. These conditions have contributed to a greater sense of connection in the world, beginning with the connection between and among larger groups of people.

Here are some of the significant benefits of globalization:

Mutual Benefit / Interdependence. Countries come together as they realize they need each other. The reasons may vary, including dependence on one another for goods and services, as well as for security and protection. Connections made through mutual dependence and interdependence add strength, resilience, and sustainability to these mutual relationships.

Trade Relationships. Connections made through trade begin as transactional; yet, may result in close friendships and interdependence. Equally, they support the full exchange of ideas, customs, and products. In a world that is connected through trade, interdependence, goodwill, and understanding, there is a natural and ongoing exchange of ideas, knowledge, and understanding. We learn from being in relationship with others. As our connections in the world expand, our collective knowledge and understanding also grows.

Diversity. Globalization has brought the world together. We connect through travel, communication, technology, and mobilization. Nations, cities, and local communities are becoming more diverse as we become more and more mobile in the modern world. This diversity enriches and strengthens communities worldwide and helps us to experience True Community wherever we go.

Compassion. The connections born of global awareness help us to better understand and accept our differences. As we open our hearts to the larger world, we see that what we share exceeds the differences we have with people from around the world. This realization opens our hearts in compassionate understanding. Compassion begins within each person; yet, nations around the world can connect in compassion and understanding as well. This is especially true when the leaders of nations worldwide choose to model and demonstrate understanding, acceptance, and compassion for all people, regardless of their nationality, ethnicity, creed, or religion.

Understanding. The expanding knowledge and awareness that results from global connections deepens our understanding of ourselves and others. This same understanding applies to nations across the world. Economic globalization brings us into contact with each other in ways that supports greater awareness and understanding of the values, goals, and vision of particular players on the world stage and people from varying cultural and socioeconomic backgrounds.

Learning and Growth. We learn and grow through new experiences. Similarly, countries learn and grow collectively as they connect globally. Connecting with others from countries around the world offers rich opportunities to expand our knowledge and awareness of these cultures. This, in turn, leads to greater acceptance and trust.

Access to New Ideas. Through our connections with other cultures and nations, we broaden our perspective and are introduced to new ways of seeing the world. When we open our hearts to others, we want to learn more about them and better understand what motivates them. In the process, new ideas and innovative practices and methods of connection are born.

The Downside of Globalization

While the growth of a global economy has resulted in a more connected world, its negative impact affects us all. These are areas that invite our deep understanding and full awareness. Each of us can consider how changes at the individual, family, and local level might lessen these negative effects. In fact, it is through our discerning actions taken at the local level that our communities will be strengthened and become more sustainable, reducing our current dependence on and support of the mega global economic system. We can also add our voice to decisions made at the collective level through our involvement in the local, regional, and national government. Here are some of the significant detriments of globalization:

Energy Consumption. Increased globalization allows for more demand coming from points across the world. This increased demand calls for increased production of goods that must be delivered quickly to those at greater distances. Because of this growing market demand, products must be moved to consumers who are scattered around the world. While this economic picture seems good for manufacturers, the environmental impact is significant. The increased energy usage required to produce, package, and move those products takes a toll on the environment and depletes reserves. The human toll must also be taken into account.

Depletion of Natural Resources. Our global economic system seems to dismiss the reality that earth's precious natural resources are limited. The prevailing mindset of those leading the global economic system is that our economic growth potential is unlimited, despite decreasing resources and other environmental impacts. This ongoing pursuit of financial gain is based on greed and profits largely for huge multinational corporations that are driven by economics without considering the impact on our earth home, including humanity. This unbridled pursuit of profit is wreaking havoc on the world around us.

Climate Change. The earth is experiencing global warming at alarming rates. Dramatic changes in our climate has led to rising temperatures and the rapid melting of arctic ice resulting in a subsequent rise of sea levels in the world's oceans. Some regions have become increasingly arid, with a lack of clean water, frequent wildfires, and increasingly intense weather events. Other parts of the globe have experienced repeated flooding and increasingly violent storms.

Corruption. Globalization has seen the unparalleled growth of many businesses across the world. Huge conglomerates now dominate the economic world. As businesses grow in size and power, the prevailing mindset often encourages companies to become larger and larger, richer and richer, leading some businesses to engage in corrupt practices in order to grow more quickly. As the demand for more products expands, businesses may exploit those who are most vulnerable, forcing women and children and other vulnerable populations to provide cheap labor in sweat shops or enter into other forms of exploitative relationships.

Greed. Over time, greed breeds power struggles and conflicts, even wars. In times of war, infrastructure may be damaged or destroyed and people displaced, injured, or killed to satisfy that desire for more. As we come to new understanding about the consequences of wasteful habits and greed, many are waking up to see that we must reverse the damage done and care for the earth. More individuals, organizations, and corporations around the world have begun to adopt more conscious practices that value natural resources. This is good news. More people are beginning to see the earth as sacred and are taking action to treat its precious gifts with greater respect and appreciation. Conscious businesses are engaging in fair trade practices that treat local producers of goods with equitable trade practices. Forced labor practices that often exploit women, children and other vulnerable groups are being called out for their blatant human rights violations. All of these are promising signs that, together, we can lessen the negative impacts of economic globalization.

Simple Ideas for Connecting with the World

World peace begins within each heart, and a more peaceful world is possible as we begin to expand our consciousness globally. Ways to cultivate meaningful global connections naturally emerge as we realize our common humanity. Our curiosity nudges us to try new experiences, consider new ways of seeing the world, and learn new languages. Each of these actions can broaden our perspective and help us to feel more connected to the greater global community. A few examples of simple ways to cultivate global connections include the following:

- giving to global humanitarian causes
- embracing the differences of persons from other cultures
- traveling to other countries to explore and discover

The threads of diversity are woven into a rich and beautiful tapestry as we connect with each other in the world. How you decide to connect with the larger world is a matter of personal choice. As with all relationships, our choices reflect our preferences, our needs, and our desires as well as our personality style, our willingness to change, and our openness for expansion.

When you open your heart to others, the possibilities are unlimited. Even though we may not speak the same language as persons in other areas of the world, we can easily connect through simple gestures, such as smiles and laughter. The universal language of the arts, to include the visual arts, music, theater, and dance, also connects us in ways verbal communication cannot.

Local Action for Global Connection

Global awareness does not mean that we have to physically travel to another country to take action and be engaged globally. We can act locally with a global awareness and perspective. Most people do not have the resources for extensive travel, and many realize the enormous energy use that such travel requires. Yet many overlook the many ways we can act locally within our own communities.

Often, actions taken in our communities do eventually influence our region, nation, and even the global community. With the global awareness that what we are doing locally also has an impact on the world, we can embrace a way of thinking and acting that embraces the underlying assumption and belief that we are all connected. Knowing our heartfelt actions in our local communities contribute to a more peaceful, harmonious, and just world, we can bring global awareness to our choices for local action.

There are many ways to cultivate global connections. The ways in which we can choose to expand our connection with our global neighbors are as varied as we are. Here are some simple ideas that might inspire your connection to the global community in ways you may not have thought of previously:

- ✓ **Be Curious.** Your curiosity about the world expands as you connect more fully with who you really are. Self-awareness inspires the desire to know and understand more. Ask your local librarian to point out books to deepen your knowledge about different cultures, languages, and ways of life. The world with its rich cultural traditions is now at your fingertips through the internet. While educating ourselves about the world online cannot replace the value of interpersonal connections, it is a great way to expand our base of knowledge about the world.

- ✓ **Learn a New Language.** Learning a second or third language allows you to connect with those who speak that language and expand your horizons. Being at least bilingual opens up doors of opportunity for you to expand and enrich your connections through conversation. Further, you may be able to assist by acting as a translator.

- ✓ **Travel.** Visiting other countries and cultures gives you opportunities to learn and expand your perspective. You will make new friends in other countries and get a firsthand look at how other cultures experience the world.

✓ **Host an Exchange Student.** Look into the possibility of hosting a student from another country through your local school system or university. These programs provide students from other cultures with learning opportunities outside their home country. Both the student and members of the host family learn from each other and make meaningful connections that bring the world closer together through mutual understanding and benefit.

✓ **Host or Attend International Events.** Celebrate the rich diversity in your local community by helping to plan or coordinate an event that highlights the various cultures of persons living around you. This event might include a potluck dinner of international foods, international dress, and international customs. Make the event a fun and educational celebration of representative cultures or focus on a single nationality or culture.

✓ **Speak Up and Take a Stand.** Speak up about social issues that you care about. Take a stand against social injustice in the world. Support organizations that address global issues you care about.

✓ **Connect Creatively.** The way of pen pals of the past has evolved into new possibilities for connection with those who live at greater distances. Explore new ways to connect with persons in other cultures through social media and videoconferencing technology.

✓ **Think Globally.** Adopt a global mindset. Think of yourself as a global citizen, connected vitally to all the world. Even though it is important to contextualize yourself in the world based on your roots and your local community, you can see yourself more expansively as being a citizen of the world. Thinking globally does not mean you give up your identity as a citizen of the country and community you call home. It means you are willing to express your inner wholeness through the ways you think and *act* in the world, to include ways that impact our shared resources and experience.

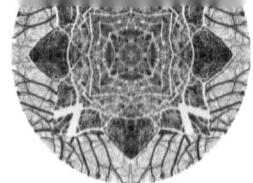

> You cannot get through a single day without having an impact on the world around you. What you do makes a difference, and you have to decide what kind of difference you want to make.
>
> Jane Goodall

Going Deeper: Connecting as a Global Citizen

THE SPIRAL PATHWAY TO DEEPENING global connection opens before you as you begin to see yourself as a citizen of the earth. The possibilities for global connection are limited only by your mind's refusal to follow your heart's desire for connection with people and ideas from around the globe. This chapter looks more closely at global connection and possibilities for inspired action arising from the desire for and awareness of global connection.

Focus Questions: *Global Connection*

Reflect on the following focus questions to return to the experience of True Community through your global connection. In your journal, write down your responses to the following three questions:

1. At this point in my life, how would I describe my connection to the world in a global sense?

2. How committed am I to going deeper on my pathway to global connection?

3. Global connection begins within each person's heart. How would I assess the love I have for myself right now?

On Being a Global Citizen

As you open to experience yourself more fully in the world, you may notice a shift in the way that you see yourself in the world. Old boundaries that once defined where you belonged in the world may have become more porous and less rigid. In your expansion, you may find it interestingly difficult to see yourself being bound by place. Your wings are unfolding. You are preparing to belong to the world in a more expansive way—as a global citizen.

As we expand our awareness of the world and understand how we fit into the world contextually, we are awakened to our personal responsibility to the global community. Our heightened sense of belonging at a global level awakens us to our responsibility to make the world a better place for all. While global awareness is fueled in part by our curiosity, openness, and heartfelt desire to connect with others, more and more people are seeing and experiencing themselves as global citizens. Global citizens act from a global awareness and an understanding of how they fit into the world. They are not satisfied to merely be aware of the world; rather, they are inspired and compelled to take responsible and discerning action to contribute to the greater good.

Though citizenship is a legal status for individuals born or naturalized into a country or nation, global citizenship is not a legal status. It is more about our sense of responsibility to take meaningful action for the whole of the world than an identifier that sets us apart from others. While those who see themselves as global citizens may view the entire world as their home and have a sense of belonging and responsibility to the larger world, their legal citizenship status is still determined by their country of birth or naturalization.

It takes each of us acting from the truth of who we really are to co-create a better world for all. Those who are global citizens may choose to act locally in ways that have global impact. Or they may take actions on the world stage. Global citizens are ever mindful of how their actions impact the world at large because they are vitally aware of how we are all connected through webs of relationships.

Global citizens are committed to a more just and equitable world for all. They understand that the basis of a more peaceful and just world is the ability to understand and accept differences and to find common ground. They know that this leads to the quicker resolution of conflicts in ways that benefit the whole.

Citizens of the World

Global citizenship is in part about how we see ourselves in relation to the larger world. It is about understanding yourself and how you fit in to the context of the larger community. If this description of global citizenship sounds similar to the general concept of global awareness, it's because the two concepts are similar in some ways. While holding global awareness is a prerequisite to identifying yourself a global citizen, you can be vastly aware from a global perspective and still not think of yourself as a global citizen.

Like those who embrace global awareness, global citizens understand their place in the world and they see that place as very important and meaningful. They are compassionate and empathetic, because they understand and value our shared humanity. Again like those with global awareness, global citizens are open-minded and embrace all of humanity and each individual citizen of the world. Even though those who see themselves in global terms may be loyal to the country where they were born or currently live, a global citizen's perspective is much broader. They see themselves first and foremost as belonging to the world. Their previously held view of how they fit into the world has shifted. The boundaries that once defined their place in the world are changing, becoming softer and less defined.

To see yourself as a global citizen opens you to new ideas and experiences. Global citizens see themselves as connected to the entire world and they see their social responsibilities including the entire world. They see beyond the confines of the boundaries of the country they call home. While they may have much pride in their home country, they see that the world extends much farther.

Global citizens have a natural curiosity about the world and so desire to engage with it in as many ways as possible, to include extended travel. Because they see the world as connected, they are interested in what is happening in the world and so they stay informed. They see that social injustice in the world affects not just those who are directly affected, but it affects the entire world. They see that as a global citizen they have certain responsibilities that begin within themselves, include their local communities and that extend to the entire world. They see themselves as citizens of the world and as stewards of the earth.

Those who are deeply connected with their True Selves naturally embrace the larger world community because they realize their oneness with it. Their creative impulse is to experience ever-expanding connections in response to their innate yearning to express fully in the world. Seeing themselves as global citizens is a mindset with which they feel comfortable. Grounded in a sense of True Community, they enjoy a strong sense of belonging at home in their local community, yet they also understand and honor their belonging in the world. They value and seek to honor their innate needs for love, belonging, contribution, meaning, and purpose and accomplish this by engaging in the world to help make it a more peaceful, just, and sustainable home for all.

Global citizens see their responsibility to take action for the greater good not only for our current world, but also for the world of tomorrow. While grounded in the present, they are future-oriented. They desire to make a difference in the world and model actions that might inspire others to expand their viewpoints.

What are your concerns for the world? How might you make a difference in the world if you would see yourself as a global citizen and take action based on that view of yourself?

A Broader Perspective

There are numerous organizations and groups worldwide that are working diligently to bring people across the world together, to strengthen global connections for a more peaceful and sustainable world. One such notable organization is the United Nations. The UN, created in 1945, is an international organization with global reach. According to its charter, the UN's work revolves around four main purposes:

1. To maintain international peace and security
2. To protect human rights
3. To deliver humanitarian aid
4. To promote sustainable development

The United Nations connects member nations of the world around these key purposes. The UN model is one example of how nations can come together to effectively address issues of global concern.

While organizations such as the UN work to strengthen connections among nations across the world, the exclusive identification with one's own nation and its interests emphasizes patriotism, pride in, and undivided loyalty to a specific nation or group within a nation. While nationalism may give some a sense of belonging and context, it may also serve to disconnect or separate adherents from a larger world view.

In the world today, separation, prejudice, intolerance, and violence toward other nations or citizens of those nations are the frequent result of unchecked nationalism. While global awareness embraces differences and looks for common ground on which to build connections among nations, nationalism tends to lead to separation.

Pause now to reflect for a few minutes on what it means to be a global citizen. Are you a global citizen? What are some changes or actions you could take to move you toward global citizenship?

Collective Global Consciousness

Our global awareness helps us determine how we see ourselves in the context of the whole world. It includes our knowledge and understanding of various cultures of the world and our choice to embrace our differences rather than allow them to separate or divide. Our global awareness expands as we open to allow more learning and understanding, which leads to a more connected and compassionate world. At its root, global consciousness is about our choice to believe that we are all connected at deeper levels of our being. It is about oneness and unity.

Growing numbers of people in the world today are coming to accept the ancient idea that we are connected at some deep level of our being. Many believe that, because we are connected, we can intentionally focus that consciousness to effect changes in the world. Science now seems to be coming closer to bearing out those ancient beliefs.

Those who adhere to the ideas of a global consciousness often believe in the energetic power of our conscious thoughts and the ways this energy can be used to impact matter, thoughts, and events in the world around us. They are giving new energy and focus to the belief in the power of prayer, meditation, contemplation, and other practices that have been used since ancient times. Closely related to the underlying idea of the power of collective consciousness is the possibility that the continued and focused energy of the collective consciousness has the power to bring about changes in the overall consciousness to reach a tipping point that will raise the consciousness level of the entire earth.

Characteristics of Global Citizens

Here are some personal attributes that are common to persons who consider themselves global citizens and who act responsibly from their expanded global perspectives:

- ✓ **Open and Accepting.** We can make more meaningful connections in the world when we express ourselves in the world with openness. Those who see themselves as global citizens are accepting and tolerant of differences among people.

- ✓ **Tolerant.** While they may not necessarily agree with other people's actions and ideas, those who choose to be global citizens are willing to give them space to be heard.

- ✓ **Curious and Informed.** Global citizens remain open and curious about the world. They are eager to learn and experience more. They realize they are empowered by information, so they keep up with current events and their impact in regions of the world.

- ✓ **Responsible.** Responsibility is a hallmark of global citizenship. Through responsible actions, positive change can occur. Global citizens have a keen sense of responsibility and are accountable for their actions.

- ✓ **Inclusive.** The beautiful tapestry woven from the rich threads of diversity of peoples and cultures leads global citizens to see all people as valuable and having intrinsic worth. Global citizens embrace all people as belonging to the world.

- ✓ **Act with Integrity.** Closely related to their sense of responsibility to the larger world, global citizens are honest in their relationships. They know that honesty builds trust. They keep their word and live up to their commitments to the best of their ability.

- ✓ **Authentic.** Global citizens have a deepening self-awareness that leads them to show up in the world with the truth of who they know themselves to be.

- ✓ **Take Action for the Greater Good.** When global citizens take action, they act responsibly, decisively, and with purpose. From their expanded perspective, they have the ability to discern the actions that will have the greatest positive impact for the world.

Pause for a few moments to reflect on this list of attributes. How many of these attributes do you have already? What are your thoughts about global citizenship? Consider choosing one of the characteristics in the list above to cultivate in the coming weeks or months.

Practices for Connection: The Global Community

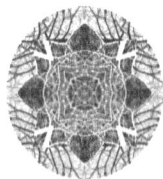

THIS CHAPTER OFFERS SOME PRACTICES to expand your awareness and experience of global connection. Refer to these practices and the questions for deeper reflection as you continue to strengthen your connection to the global community in the coming months and years.

Connecting to the Global Community

Take a few minutes to reflect on your current level of engagement with the world. How does it feel?

Being connected globally is a state of being that involves our being open to new ways of experiencing the world outside our usual experiences. While we can gain much knowledge about other cultures around the world from books and movies, actually experiencing diverse cultures and ways of life can be most meaningful and powerful. Your experiences are enriched when you approach them with curiosity, openness to learn something new, acceptance, and open-heartedness.

This chapter offers some varied ways you can broaden your experience of global connection. Use these ideas to get a taste of the satisfaction that can come from being connected globally. The experiences that these practices offer can serve as springboards to other creative ways you can deepen your experience of being wholly connected along the pathway of connection to the global community.

> ✓ **Take a Personal Stand on a Global Issue.** Select a specific global issue that speaks to you. Research the issue to learn as much about it as you can. You may find information from reliable online resources, from your public library, or the news media. Your thorough research is one way to become informed on the issue. Empower yourself with reliable information. From your research and from your inner wisdom, form an opinion

on the issue. Determine what actions you might take on the issue from your empowered and informed position.

- ✓ **Taste the World.** This practice helps you expand your experience of the world locally through eating. Identify restaurants in your local town or a nearby community that specializes in ethnic foods. Set an intention to visit at least one of these restaurants once a month or as your budget allows. The purpose of this practice is to familiarize you with international cuisine. When you visit, be curious about ingredients, food preparation methods, and the origin of the food and traditions around it.

- ✓ **Connect with a Pen Pal.** Look online for reputable pen pal websites that can connect you to new friends around the world. By connecting with a pen pal, you can expand your global awareness about people, cultures, language, and more. You may want to start with one pen pal and over time connect with additional pen pals to expand your connections in the world.

- ✓ **Visit a Local International Market.** If traveling to another country is not feasible for you, locate and visit an international market in your town or nearby city. As you walk through the shops in the marketplace, enjoy a full experience through your senses. Notice the colors of foods, clothing, and decorative items. Smell the aromas of foods and spices. Take time to sample various foods or eat a meal. Notice the sounds and pay attention to languages you hear. Touch the textures of fabrics and other items for sale in shops. As you take in the market, notice what feelings are coming up for you. Do you feel open and curious? Whatever you are feeling in the moment is ok. Meet yourself where you are. If possible, purchase a small item as a gift to yourself for your willingness to expand your cultural awareness.

✓ **Travel Internationally.** This practice may not be feasible for everyone because of a variety of factors, including the cost of travel. For those who can travel, seeing the world up close is one of the best ways to really experience global connections. There are creative ways to see the world on a smaller budget. You might consider traveling with a group of friends or with an organized travel group that allows you to make new connections. Set the intention to see the world; then explore cost-effective and creative ways to do just that. Capture your experiences and observations through photographs and travel journaling.

✓ **Become an International Chef for a Night.** Express yourself creatively by preparing an international meal for your family or a group of friends. Researching the recipes and ingredients can be an interesting and fun experience. Purchase the foods and ingredients from an international market if possible. Share what you have learned with your family or guests as you enjoy the meal. As an ongoing practice, you might consider preparing a meal each month from a different country or ethnic group.

✓ **Music of the World.** Music is a universal way to connect with others. We open ourselves to understand others more deeply when we take the time to learn about their customs, to include musical styles and tradition. For this practice, choose four countries that interest you. Research their music online or at your public library. If you have the technology capacity, create a playlist of music representative of each of the countries. During a one-month period, listen to the music from each county for period of one week. Simply listen to the music, experiencing the culture through the music. As you listen to the music, notice how you feel. What is your experience of this music of the world? In your journal, write about your experience, noting feelings, thoughts, and insights that arose as you listened to the music.

21 Questions for Deeper Reflection

1. How does my connection with my True Self contribute to my embracing the whole world?
2. In what ways am I a global citizen?
3. How does my perception of myself as a global citizen impact the ways I show up in the world?
4. What are some practical ways I can connect more fully with the world?
5. What is the importance of my connecting globally?
6. How does my seeing the intrinsic value in all people enhance my experience of global connection?
7. How willing am I to step into the experience of cultures that are different from my native culture?
8. How can my local community benefit from my deepening global awareness?
9. What is my willingness to learn a new language?
10. How might my worldview and experiences change if I invest in the time to learn a new language?
11. In what ways can I contribute to cultural awareness in my local community?
12. How might an international celebration in my local community contribute to a more compassionate community?
13. How can my openness and curiosity enrich my travel experiences in the world?
14. Reflect on any deep-seated prejudices, beliefs, or assumptions that you hold about other ethnic or cultural groups. How willing are you to let those go?
15. How willing am I to take a stand on a global issue I feel strongly about?

16. How are my personal values reflected in how I connect with the larger world?

17. What is one personal action I can take to promote acceptance of differences among people in the world?

18. What is important to me about being connected to the world?

19. What is one action I can take to contribute to world peace?

20. How can I open my heart and come more fully to those in my neighborhood who look different from me or who come from different cultural or ethnic backgrounds?

21. How connected to the world do I feel? Do I feel a sense of belonging from a global perspective?

In Closing: **An Invitation to Opening**

THIS BOOK'S CLOSING does not signal an ending. Rather, it offers a point of beginning anew. Nature unfolds from the center, expanding to its fullest expression; then, just as naturally, it folds back in upon itself, only to repeat the cycle of unfolding again from center and closing back in, according to the creative impulse of life's expression. Rather than an ending, let these closing thoughts be a warm and heartfelt invitation to step fully into the experience of your own unfolding in the world.

If this book has fulfilled its purpose, it has inspired you on your personal journey to the experience of True Community. As we have traveled along the five pathways of The Spiral Path, we have explored aspects of what it means to enter into and experience community. We began at the center, with the heart of who you are—your innermost self or the True Self. Spiraling outward from here, the remaining four pathways led us to a deeper sense of purpose and belonging in community. These are the pathways of connection to family and friends, the larger community, nature, and the global community.

The questions and practices for reflection and action included in each of the five sections of this book will support you in moving toward a wholly connected life that is a reflection of True Community, an inner state of being that naturally expands outward. As you return to them, these practices will support you in anchoring to each of the five pathways. As you deepen your connection along each of these pathways, you support the experience of True Community for all.

As we connect deeper along The Spiral Path, life invites us to a fuller participation with it. While the realization of wholeness brings inner and outer satisfaction, the continuous evolution and change occurring in the world around you reminds you that there is always more to experience and express. Your inner creative spark, which is your truth, nudges you to deepen your connection by stepping into ever fuller expression of your True Self in the world. The choice of how you express your truth is yours alone. The outer manifestation of your being will be determined by how you choose to participate in the world.

The arc of your journey is your personal choice, and only you can decide how you connect with the world around you. The choice before you is whether you will step into the full unfolding of your life. Will you allow yourself to be wholly connected to your True Self, to your family and friends, to your local community, to nature, and to the global community? Or will you choose a life of disconnection and separation?

A choice to live a contracted and constricted version of yourself is a choice to withhold from the world the fullest expression of your True Self. The world cannot be at its fullness without your integral magnificence expressing in it. What will be your choice?

Acknowledgments

To my editor and friend, Dawn Richerson, for your unwavering support as this book took shape and form. Without your clarity, creativity, inspiration, and gentle nudging this book would still be an idea in the great field of possibility. Thank you also for your artistic rendering of The Spiral of Connection that brings to lovely form the concepts on which this book is based.

To my brother Ken Callaway for the generous contribution of your mandala artwork that graces the book, both inside and out. Also, thank you and your artist wife (and my sister-in-law) Judy for providing your insights and creative inspiration for the entire project.

To Hilary Smith for providing your keen insights along the way and for keeping this book project on track. You smoothed our way forward with your attention to detail and your dedication to the successful completion of the entire project.

To the board of directors of True Center for your ongoing support of our organizational vision and mission. Without your guidance and inspiration True Center and this book would not be a reality in the world.

To our entire True Center community for your ongoing support of our programming and services in our local community and the world. May our heartfelt connections through True Center enrich the expansive experience of True Community in the world.

To my entire family whose unwavering love and support have always guided and inspired my unfolding. Thank you especially to Casey, Hilary, and Barrett.

About True Center

Deeply rooted in the fabric of the local community, True Center provides a welcoming space to remember who you are, reclaim your voice of truth, and restore your connection to wholeness. We serve as a connector for individuals and groups committed to working together to create a more harmonious, peace-filled community.

True Center supports a thriving local community through:

- Evidence-based training, education, programs and workshops
  for individuals and groups.

- Go-to resources and ready-made programs for organizations committed to social and community transformation.

- A forum for vital conversations that contribute to a more compassionate community.

We would love to connect with you. Reach us by email at admin@truecenterwoodstock.org. To learn more about programs and services visit our website at www.truecenterwoodstock.org.

About the Author

Eve Callaway Willson, MSW, CPC, is a social worker and certified professional coach. She retired after a long career in public sector social services and behavioral health and then began the next phase of her life as a consultant, coach, and connector.

As founder and executive director of True Center, an educational nonprofit organization, Eve continues to pursue her passion to support others in remembering who they really are so they can live full and meaningful lives as contributors to thriving and compassionate communities. She believes in a return to true community one heart at a time.

Eve is a mother and grandmother. She lives in Woodstock, Georgia.

www.ingramcontent.com/pod-product-compliance
Lightning Source LLC
Chambersburg PA
CBHW030324080526
44584CB00012B/693